BECOME A PROPERTY MILLIONAIRE IN YOUR $PARE TIME

How to get started as a <u>successful</u> property investor.
GUARANTEED.

Mark Kelman

First published in 2014 by Major Street Publishing Pty Ltd
PO Box 106, Highett, Vic. 3190.
Contact: info@majorstreet.com.au
© Mark Kelman 2014

The moral rights of the author have been asserted.
National Library of Australia Cataloguing-in-Publication data:

Author:	Kelman, Mark, author.
Title:	Become a property millionaire in your spare time: How to get started as a successful property investor
ISBN:	9780987542915
Subjects:	Real estate investment--Popular works.
	Investments--Popular works.
	Real property--Management--Popular works.
	Finance, Personal--Popular works.
Dewey Number:	332.6324

All rights reserved. Except as permitted under the Australian Copyright Act 1968 (for example, a fair dealing for the purposes of study, research, criticism or review), no part of this book may be reproduced, stored in a retrieval system, communicated or transmitted in any form or by any means without prior written permission. All inquiries should be made to the publisher.

Cover design by Penny Black Design
Internal design by Production Works
Printed in Australia by Griffin Press
10 9 8 7 6 5 4 3 2 1

Disclaimer: The material in this publication is of in the nature of general comment only, and neither purports nor intends to be advice. Readers should not act on the basis of any matter in this publication without considering (and if appropriate taking) professional advice with due regard to their own particular circumstances. The author and publisher expressly disclaim all and any liability to any person, whether a purchaser of this publication or not, in respect of anything and the consequences of anything done or omitted to be done by any such person in reliance, whether whole or partial, upon the whole or any part of the contents of this publication.

Guarantee: We guarantee to show you how to get started as a successful property investor. If after having read this entire book, you don't believe that this book has done this, and if you contact us in writing at enquiries@achieveproperty.com, with proof of purchase, within 12 months of buying the book, and request a refund then we will happily refund the cost of the book that you paid. We cannot guarantee that you will be a success or that you will become a property millionaire – that is up to you!

FOREWORD BY STEVE McKNIGHT

So, you want to be a property millionaire, do you?

Well, it's definitely still possible – even after one of the biggest booms in real estate prices Australia has ever seen. Sure, it won't be easy, but with the right education and some clever pointers from those with relevant experience, you'll be well positioned to profit.

Mark Kelman is certainly a person you can learn a lot from, especially if you're a new investor and are seeking practical information. Mark has earned his investing stripes the old fashioned way, by starting with nothing but desire, and via hard work, forging success by turning problems into solutions.

Truth be told, Mark is just the sort of person you should learn from because his experience is recent, and that makes it relevant and replicable.

Which brings me to this excellent book. In it you'll find a clever combination of investing theory and practical application, written sensibly and sequentially to explain how to build an impressive property portfolio, right from the start.

I only wish a book such as this had existed when I began investing. I'm certain it would have fast tracked my success by helping to avoid costly rookie errors while delivering the confidence necessary to combat the fears that hold back, and providing the courage needed to take action.

At the very least, *Become a Property Millionaire in Your Spare*

Time will alert you to, and answer, technical investing questions that are tricky to solve. However, I strongly suspect you'll glean much more, and in only a matter of pages you'll agree the investment you've made to acquire this book will assist you to reach your wealth creation goals, sooner and with less effort.

STEVE MCKNIGHT
www.PropertyInvesting.com
#1 best selling author. Professional investor.
Expert property educator.

ABOUT THE AUTHOR

Mark Kelman is a young philanthropist, property investor, scientist and teacher.

At 34 years of age, and with a career path reading like an obscure menu, Mark's work has ranged from fast-food kitchenhand, to veterinary surgeon in clinical practice, to technical manager in animal health, to real estate entrepreneur, businessman and teacher. Most of the time, while working, Mark is simultaneously managing a lucrative property investing portfolio and helping others learn how to do the same.

In Mark's other spare time, he is also a keen runner completing the odd marathon and half-marathon and he actively works with a number of charities.

In Sydney, Mark runs the Sydney Property Meeting Group and his company, Achieve Property, provides training and resources for property investors, especially those starting out. For more information, visit **www.achieveproperty.com.au**.

WHAT THE PROPERTY-INVESTING INDUSTRY IS SAYING...

"Mark Kelman has achieved more in just a few short years than most property investors achieve in a lifetime, using intelligent strategies to acquire multiple properties quickly. This book is a must-read for anyone wanting to make the best possible start in property investing."

SIMON BUCKINGHAM
Professional Investor, Mentor and Director of
ResultsMentoring.com

"More money coming in than money going out is the key to successful property investing. Some call it creating a cash machine, others call it positive cash flow. Mark calls it positive gearing. And in his book, Mark proves beyond reasonable doubt, that it is the secret to building a property portfolio."

ANTHONY J. CORDATO
Property Lawyer

"Mark is what I call a "serial investor". He is highly active and determined when it comes to investing in property... He is very successful and his book shares his passion and offers great insights for anyone considering a property investment."

DAVE PHILIPSEN
Founder and Director, Rhino Money

CONTENTS

Dedication and acknowledgments **viii**
Preface **ix**

1. Journey's End – the beginning of property investing success **1**
2. Why invest in property? **11**
3. So what's holding you back? **21**
4. Finding enough money to get started in your spare time **25**
5. Securing enough finance **38**
6. Finding enough time to invest **49**
7. Understanding interest rates **58**
8. House prices and housing markets **67**
9. Valuing a property **82**
10. Landlording and managing tenants **88**
11. Making money from property investing **99**
12. Searching for and finding the right property **114**
13. The importance of thorough due diligence **124**
14. Servicing your loan **133**
15. Structuring how you purchase investment property **139**
16. Accounting, book-keeping and tax **149**
17. Learning the techniques to invest in property **160**
18. Buying your first investment property – step-by-step **169**

Conclusion **189**
Answers to quiz questions **191**
Bonus tools **193**
Index **194**

DEDICATION AND ACKNOWLEDGMENTS

This book is dedicated to all property investors – experienced and novices alike.

Investing (like any business venture) is a journey of self-discovery, and we meet many people along this path. Enjoy the journey.

A sincere thanks to everyone who helped contribute to the content of this book. Your assistance in the months of preparation and editing, after years of gathering the information and knowledge that fill the pages that follow, is much appreciated.

A special thanks to Bryan and Jacquie Kelman for thorough proof-reading, and thanks to all my family and friends for their ongoing support in all my ventures. I wouldn't have done any of this without you, and it certainly wouldn't have been as much fun. Thank you to Steve McKnight for his guidance and mentoring along my investing journey, and in life, and for writing the foreword to this book. Thanks also to my publisher Lesley Williams for her time and effort in making this book what it is today.

Lastly, to Smokey the cat, thanks for your support and, at times, the assistance with the typing.

PREFACE

Getting started in property investing isn't easy. Many people try it, though few actually succeed in creating a sizeable property portfolio that delivers the freedom and returns that they initially envisaged. Some people do manage to figure out the system and they go on to achieve property investing success. After investing in property for 10 years, and growing several sizeable portfolios, I've learnt a lot about how property investing *really* works and I would like to share these learnings with you in this book.

The reality is that you CAN grow a multi-million dollar property portfolio, without quitting your day job (in fact, keeping your job will help). I have managed to do all my investing in my spare time, fitting it in around holding several jobs.

There is a lot of misinformation around about property investing, and starting off on the wrong foot can significantly impede your progress as a property investor. Not only may it take longer to grow your portfolio, but also you risk losing large sums of money, or worse still, missing out on making money. Start out the right way and you can quickly start growing your portfolio and building your wealth.

So many people have such bad first experiences when they start investing in property that they give up before they have even properly begun. I don't want this to happen to anyone.

Every property investor has to start from somewhere, and most of us start from nothing. Over the last 10 years I have met many successful investors and many more people who are still trying to get started. Those who do manage to figure out *their way* of investing in the property market (and there are many ways) and those who stick at it, discover a world of rewarding challenges that gives great satisfaction, as well as financial benefits.

Now, I firmly believe that property investing is a skill that has to be *learnt,* it can't just be *taught,* but if you have the right teacher, and start with the right lessons, this makes learning a lot easier. You do have to take responsibility for the learning, however, no one is going to do this for you.

This book is written for people who are beginning their property investing – either you don't own any property yet but you would like to, or you own one house or a few houses, but you aren't really getting the growth or profit that you would like. If you aren't yet making at least $100,000 a year in capital growth or capital gains from property, then this book is a good start for you.

People often ask me for property investing advice, or what they should do to get started in investing. My first suggestion is to read as much as you can to be comfortable with the idea of buying your first property, then start taking action. You need to get used to spending money on education as well as property assets – if you do, you will reap much more than you sow. I also recommend that you play Robert Kiyosaki's game Cashflow® regularly (more about that in Chapter Seventeen).

By the end of this book, I hope that you are equipped with enough knowledge to buy your first couple of houses or, at the very least, you know what you need to do to be ready for your first purchases. And then do it.

One tip I will give you is to take notes at conferences you attend, at meetings and, generally, in life (and this applies to when you are reading this book too). While you are reading, some things will resonate with you. Some points will jump out at you as good ideas, or as being something you might want to implement or change. When you get these ideas, write them down immediately, either in a notebook you carry around with you, or on the notepad app on your Smartphone, or in the notes pages at the end of each chapter of this book. (If you are borrowing this book from the library or a friend, write somewhere other than in the book! – or buy your own copy to write in.) Then, when you have finished, review your notes and make a decision to put into action the things on your list (even if they don't seem as significant any more). Set a date to do them. These little changes or ideas will be the things that change your world for the better. You will be surprised. This strategy has worked for me, and many successful people before me. The vitally important thing is to take action – this is one of the keys to success.

The first three chapters in this book introduce you to property investing and what it's all about. The following fourteen chapters cover specific areas of property investing that you will need to master in order to be successful and build your own million-dollar property portfolio in your spare time. The final chapter then takes you step-by-step through successfully buying your first property.

Property investing is an interesting journey and you will learn a lot about yourself along the way. Ultimately, being successful in property will allow you the freedom to do the things you want to do.

So let's get started.

MARK KELMAN

1

JOURNEY'S END – THE BEGINNING OF PROPERTY INVESTING SUCCESS

- *Educate yourself about property investing*
- *Don't spend too much on your first property purchase*
- *Just get started!*

With the focus of this book being getting started in property investing, why don't I start by sharing my story with you on how I got into property investing. My story, at least in the beginning, started the same as everyone else's.

Like many people, I knew that I didn't want to work for someone else my whole life. I was (and still am) passionate about my work. I am fortunate to have had several jobs since graduating, and I've loved all of them. My work outside of investing is predominantly in animal welfare and science, but I also spend time on charity work and doing things I feel are positive in the world. I have always thought that I could do more if I wasn't working full time and if I had a better source of income. I found this source to be income from property investing.

When I started considering investing, having just graduated from university, I had no real savings. My degree didn't qualify me as a property investor and I wasn't earning an enormous salary from my occupation. So getting started in property investing was not going to be easy.

I had known for some time that I wanted to give investing in property a go, but I had no idea how to go about it (other than to start saving). About three years into my first job, one Christmas, I was flying home to Perth and happened to buy a book on property investing at the airport. It wasn't the first book on property that I'd read, but it did have a profound impact on me. This was the book that would start to shape my property investing career. It was then that I made the decision to really get going in property. I decided to read as much as I could on investing then when I was ready I would buy the best property I could (with my current knowledge) to just get started.

At the height of the property boom on the east coast of Australia, in 2004, I started investing in property. This may sound like bad timing but with my strategy I was able to find profitable deals even at this time when everyone else was saying, "You should have been looking four years ago".

The positive cash flow approach

The book I had been reading suggested I look for positive cash flow property. With this approach, you seek out property to buy as an investment, the income from which pays for all expenses related to buying and managing the property and provides you with some income on top. The expenses covered include the cost of the interest on the mortgage, council rates, insurances, repairs, property management, etc.). This sounded great to me. It is the opposite of negative gearing, where you make a loss from your property and you can offset this loss against other taxable income – which never made sense to me.

I began scouring the internet for high-yielding properties around Sydney that would be cash flow positive – only to come up with blanks. Not to be put off, I kept searching for several months, still with no results. So I figured I would look a little further afield. I checked out Newcastle and Wollongong and again came up with nothing at the time.

Then a real estate agent from Wollongong who I had been talking to suggested I try the New England area (around Tamworth, home of Australian country music and the giant guitar). He was of the opinion that property in this region fetched higher rents. I did some research and uncovered a few towns that looked as if they might have potential for growth. A few months later I was in the area, physically inspecting a number of houses, one of which was to become my first investment property.

In the area I had chosen there were several towns in the vicinity of Tamworth. My logic at the time was that Tamworth was a large regional centre and these peripheral towns (provided they were of a reasonable size) would also offer fairly good investments. Mining was starting up in the area and it was an agricultural region with plenty of retail businesses. There were also various developments and infrastructure plans in the pipeline and in construction phase. The towns I was looking at all had their own supermarkets, most had fast-food outlets and they seemed to be doing OK. I figured these were signs that the local economies were fairly strong.

With my girlfriend at the time, I visited real estate agencies in several towns. We looked at real estate listings in windows and spoke to agents. We drove around a lot!

We had seen quite a few properties that the agents had said would have high rents and a low enough purchase price so that the rent could pay off the mortgage interest and expenses (making it cash flow positive). However, we weren't sure, given the condition of some of the properties, if they were really habitable or if the cost of repairs might make buying them not worth investing in.

Getting close to my first purchase

One property I had seen in an agent's window was in good condition in Barraba, a small town with a population of 1,200. The asking price on this house was $60,000 and it would rent for $125 a week. I wasn't quite ready to buy in this town but I knew I was on the right track and that positive cash flow properties could be found.

I had decided that a town I was keen on was Quirindi (pronounced Ku-rin-die), with a population of 2,600. It was about 100 km south of Tamworth and there was a lot of local council rezoning, resulting in the town becoming a regional centre for the district. I'll never know if this played any role in the appreciation of the local market but it seemed as if it might at the time.

So after a few days of looking at properties, and on the way home to Sydney, I decided to try one more agent, Nick from Quirindi, who had quite a few listings that roughly fitted my criteria for the amount of rent needed to make the property cash flow positive.

Nick started by showing me a few properties of a similar standard to those I had already seen – most of these houses must have been over a hundred years old, and while they had stood the test of time, they were showing their age. I wasn't an experienced investor back then but even I could tell that when a floor had a significant slope there were going to be structural repairs needed to fix it.

Just as I was giving up hope, the last house that Nick took us to was in slightly better shape than the rest. It was on a large block (2,000 m^2) and still old but in reasonable condition. It had three bedrooms and three sleep-outs, so it commanded a reasonably high rent and it was certainly the best house I had seen on the whole trip.

The price that was being asked for it was $105,000 so it seemed affordable. The rent I could get from it was $155 a week. With interest rates at the time at 7%, this would be approximately cash flow neutral.

It certainly wasn't a palace. The house was made of timber with an iron roof and it had aluminium cladding stuck over the pre-existing weatherboards. There was a shed in the backyard that looked older than the house (if that were possible). It was on a corner block (which I thought was good) and also had a second block, part of the 2,000 m² land, on a separate title. I thought this might also be of interest when it came time to sell.

I did my property inspection as best as I could. The floors were roughly level, the house seemed in reasonable condition, and there were no glaringly obvious faults that I could see.

Being the best house we had seen, and in line with my plan to buy the best property I could with the knowledge I had to get into the market, I decided to submit an offer. After all, the goal of the trip was to buy a house and get started in investing.

Not knowing anything about negotiating, or valuing houses, I decided to offer $15,000 less than the vendor (seller) was asking, and made an offer of $90,000. With experience now, I have a much different approach to establishing the true value of an investment, but at the time, this was all I knew.

One interesting thing to keep in mind is that buying your first house will most likely be the scariest investment you make. So many things go through your mind as you prepare to buy this first property: what happens if interest rates go sky-high, what if it catches on fire, what if you did your calculations wrong? Your first million-dollar property will probably not feel as scary as your first-ever purchase. But you only get to buy your first house once, so enjoy it.

The agent came back with a counter-offer from the vendor of $100,000. I counter-offered again at $94,000. We eventually agreed on $96,000, and I remember the excitement of successfully negotiating my first-*ever* investment property.

Here's a photo of the property below.

My first investment property, purchased in Quirindi, NSW in 2004

Caught by the property bug

A few months after buying and settling on that property, I went back to Barraba and bought the other house for $53,000. My second investment property was a 1930s, ex-housing commission home in the south of town. Housing commission homes back then were really well built and this house had been owner-occupied for many years. It was a two-bedroom weatherboard and iron home on a large block in need of some renovation. But it was very sturdy and had character. I could see myself one day retiring to the country and living happily there (though I've since sold it). The name of that house was "Journey's End"!

'Journey's End', purchased in Barraba, NSW in 2004

In the space of a couple of months I'd bought not one but two investment properties – and I had a lot more to learn. However, I'd made a start and this was the beginning of my first property investment portfolio. Having bought these two houses, I had reached my first ceiling where I didn't know what to do next. So, for the time being, I could not buy any more property.

I spent the next two years reading, learning, attending seminars and managing these properties while I climbed my way to the next level. Having just started in investing, I'd bought two houses that were cash flow neutral or positive but I had no idea how to add good capital value to these deals. Through education and experience I now have a much better system for profiting from day one – which we will cover later.

With hindsight

From this slow beginning, my investments have grown to a portfolio valued at millions of dollars. The reality is anyone can achieve the same. In fact, with education and the right start, and the information you will find in this book, you may progress considerably faster than I did.

The property market has changed since I purchased my initial two houses. If anything, these sorts of property deals are now easier to find. Again, this will make it much easier for first-time investors to get into the market, if they know what they are looking for. Even though the media perennially talk about a "housing shortage" and even though people say you cannot find properties with cash flow and good capital gains potential, you can. You need the right tools and you need to know what you are looking for. However, good deals don't stay on the market for long, and these properties will not be around forever, so now is the time to get started. And when you find a good deal, don't waste time – buy it!

I made numerous mistakes in buying these first two houses but making mistakes is the second-best way of learning. Learning from other people's mistakes is a far better way of learning!

Looking back, one thing I did right was to just get started – because most people fail having never even tried.

Both of these properties I have since sold and made around $50,000 profit on each of them. That's not bad for properties that cost between $50,000 and $100,000 to buy.

The second thing I did right was to not buy too big on my first deal. The first property deals you do will probably be the worst property deals you make, and the ones where you are likely to make the most mistakes. So buying something smaller should limit the risks you take from inexperience.

Above all else, the lesson here is to educate yourself about property investing, then buy the best property you can with your current knowledge and get into the market – it's the only way to get experience.

CHAPTER SUMMARY

Buying your first investment property can be a daunting experience. In fact, it should be! There is a lot of money involved in buying a property and there are risks. However, you should not let that stop you from getting started in investing.

You cannot succeed in anything that you don't start. But you should take a sensible approach when starting this kind of venture for the first time.

Tips for getting started the right way:

- **Start small and grow** – don't over-commit to a deal that is too big for your very first one (this might mean buying outside a capital city).
- **Make your mistakes on the smaller deals** – everyone makes mistakes, better to learn on the small projects where your losses will be less.
- **Learn from other people's mistakes** – this is even better than learning from your own, and a lot less costly.
- **Get educated then just take action** – educate yourself so that you are comfortable to get started, then get into the market. You need to get your feet wet at some stage and there is no better time than the present.

CHAPTER NOTES AND ACTIONS

Before moving on to the next chapter, spend a few minutes writing down the things that resonated with you from this chapter.

What actions do you need to take, or what do you need to plan to do, to help you get to the next level in your investing?

Write down at least 5 things now.

1. _____

_____

_____

2. _____

_____

_____

3. _____

_____

_____

4. _____

_____

_____

5. _____

_____

_____

2

WHY INVEST IN PROPERTY?

- *There are pros and cons associated with investing in property*
- *Property stacks up as a better investment than shares*
- *The positives of property investing outweigh the negatives.*

These days there are so many things you can invest in, so why is property still so popular? For many property investors there is just a natural attraction to owning property, for others there are clearly defined advantages that they are seeking that property provides. Following the significant impact of the global financial crisis (GFC) on share prices, and the continuing volatility of the sharemarket in Australia and overseas, it's not surprising that property is gaining popularity over traditional share investing.

A quick look at the perceived drawbacks of property

Before we start looking at the advantages in property, let's quickly look at some of the negatives, or constraints, of property investing, so that we are taking a realistic view about what we are getting into. Many of these perceived disadvantages are double-sided, that is they may seem to be a negative but they can also be a positive. Investors who are educated and knowledgeable may well be able to capitalise on these disadvantages rather than worry about them.

It may be that some of these things are what are holding you back from getting started in investing. If so, read on, as we work through the hurdles of property investing. Keep reminding yourself that hundreds of thousands of people invest in property in Australia every year. A much smaller percentage do it well!

If they can do it, so can you.

We are going to cover the negatives first, but rest assured, the positives far outweigh the negatives!

Property is slow-moving

One of the first things about property is that it is slow-moving. If you are investing and waiting for the market to move, in order to make your capital gains, then you may be waiting some time (probably years). If you time it right and invest during an upturn in the market, then you may get the added benefit of capital growth on top of the value you get from your strategies. What I mean here is that you will aim to add value to the property yourself using various techniques that we discuss later, but you will get added capital gains that the market also provides, during some stages of the property market.

Don't make the mistake of waiting until the market starts to move before getting in. By waiting, you may time your entry too late and miss out on good growth. You are also delaying the start of your investment journey and learning the skills of investing. Those who benefit most from property market movements are the seasoned investors who understand the market and are set to capitalise on opportunities as they present.

Property is a high-cost asset

Another factor of property investing is that property is a high-cost asset. Compared to shares, and even some businesses, property can be costly. You are generally looking at spending many tens of thousands of dollars for the very cheapest property, usually one to two hundred thousand dollars, even at the lower range of the market. For people starting with limited capital (cash) this may be a constraint to getting quickly into property investing.

Property is not a liquid asset

Here's a bit of investing jargon: property is not a 'liquid' asset. Liquidity represents how easy an investment is to buy and sell. Shares are considered highly liquid, as they can generally be bought and sold in an instant on the stock market. Shares can be bought and sold within a day (in fact multiple times per day if you wish). Property in Australia typically takes three months to buy and at least as long to sell (often longer). People wanting to sell property any more quickly have little choice but to discount the price. The advantage here is if you are a buyer, and you are in a position to buy a property that someone needs to sell fast, then you may be able to negotiate a discount if you can meet their needs.

Property has a high cost of entry (and exit)

Property has higher entry and exit fees than other investments, i.e. your purchasing and selling costs are significant. As well as the higher cost of the asset itself, properties have other fees you need to pay, examples include:

- **Stamp duty at purchase:** this can be between 3.5% and 5% of the purchase price, depending on in which state the property is situated in Australia and the price of the property;
- **Legal/conveyancing fees:** around $1,500 at purchase and again at sale;

- **Pest and building inspection at purchase:** between $500 and $800;
- **Agent's commission at sale:** this varies from 1.5% to 4.5%, the higher the value of the property, the lower the commission percentage, which stands to reason.

Property has management costs

There are costs involved in managing an investment property too. Unlike other forms of investment, property needs to be managed and maintained. Costs of ownership include the following:

- **Management fees:** these are generally between 5.5% to 6.6% of the rental income. This is the cost of a property manager;
- **Insurance premiums:** these vary, they are roughly 1% of the value of the property for full landlord's insurance;
- **Maintenance and repairs:** if work needs to be done on plumbing, painting, pest control, etc., this is the responsibility of the landlord. Set aside $1,000 or so for this per year. Again, costs vary depending on the property. If you don't spend it, even better, but at least you have budgeted for it;
- **Utilities:** these include electricity, water, gas and telephone. The great news is that in most cases, the tenant will be responsible for electricity, gas and telephone (and also for the costs of setting-up billing for these). Water rates are billed to the owner of the property, and in some cases the landlord will pay these. My advice is to always pass this cost on to the tenant directly. If you need to activate these before a tenant moves in, be sure to disconnect them immediately that the tenants occupy the property, and have them take over these costs straightaway.

> **HOT TIP FOR INVESTORS**
> Pass on the cost of water to the tenant directly, don't include this in the cost of rent. When a landlord gets a water bill, this can be paid and then the tenant charged for the water on top of their rent (check your state's regulations regarding this). As tenant water usage varies, you won't then be out of pocket if they take long showers!

Tenants are the most important part of property investing, as the rent they are paying is paying for your asset. But managing tenants can seem to some to be yet another 'hassle' of investing. Sometimes they don't pay the rent, and maybe leave a bit of damage when they move out. This needs to be managed as well.

These drawbacks may seem quite challenging. There are quite a few things property investors need to consider and manage, but the upside, if you invest successfully, is significant potential for profit. Property can be a very rewarding investment. So let's now look at the positives.

The positives of property investing

Having considered the perceived negatives (which keep a lot of people out of investing), we can now examine the positives – after all, there are still a lot of very successful investors out there, so there must be some benefits, right?

You don't have to manage it yourself

Firstly, if the last few pages were putting you off, don't be alarmed. One of the benefits of property investing is that the process is highly 'automatable'. By this I mean that you can get other people to manage the majority of the day-to-day running of your property, so you don't need to do it all yourself. Better still, your rental income should pay for the costs of property management, which are also tax deductible, so it won't usually cost you anything out of your own pocket.

Property is a secure asset

One of the biggest benefits of property, especially given the current volatility of the economy, is the security of the investment – the expression "Safe as houses" couldn't be more true.

As property investment assets are real physical dwellings, they cannot go into receivership and are not subject to the same market forces as shares. I've never heard of a residential property investor who got a 'margin call' (i.e. was forced to sell to reduce his exposure to debt) on their property loans. Provided you buy in an area where there is demand, and so long as there is forecast future demand, your asset will provide a safe and secure investing option. And there is also insurance for anything that can go wrong.

The property market is resilient

Along similar lines, another benefit of property is its resilience. The property market has less fluctuations than other markets, mainly due to the entry and exit costs and also the high number of people who hold on to their properties for a longer period of time. Most people don't suddenly need to sell, or suddenly want to sell, so prices stay relatively stable. Also, as there is a general undersupply of property in Australia (i.e. there are more people wanting to buy than sell) so prices will trend upwards over time.

Because of these two factors – security and resilience – lending institutions are usually happy to lend on residential property, meaning you have the benefit of leverage. This means that you can use a smaller amount of your own money and buy a property asset worth considerably more with the help of a bank's money.

As the value of the property goes up, but the loan stays the same (or goes down), you make the profit. The higher the leverage you can access, the more assets you are able to buy. In share trading you would not be able to get a 90% or 95% loan, but this is not only possible, it is also common, with property investing.

Property investing is scalable

Another benefit of investing in property is its scalability. This means that once you have a strategy in place, you can replicate the process multiple times and get the same outcome, therefore multiplying your portfolio. One of the keys to success as an investor is to work out a strategy to buy a property, make it profitable then free up your cash to repeat the process. If you can do this, you can build a million-dollar portfolio in your spare time!

Long-term high performance

The property market also shows consistently high performance, showing strong capital growth consistently over decades (even hundreds of years). We discuss price trends later in this book, suffice to say here that a major benefit of property is the potential for significant capital growth, with the safety and security discussed above.

True property market crashes are very uncommon. In the sharemarket, people can lose significant amounts of money very quickly when the market crashes. Share investors talk about "staircases and elevators" as the sharemarket moves slowly up – as if climbing stairs – but drops suddenly when it falls – like going down in a lift. Share investors quickly forget their big losses as the market returns to slow increases again and some capital is recovered, but the falls can bring very real and immediate losses. The property market doesn't behave with the same disregard for investors' capital!

Demand for property is high

In Australia, there is high demand for property. Despite lobbying for many years from groups such as the Real Estate Institutes in each state, low housing construction has continued to ensure an undersupply of property, thereby maintaining strong demand. While there is demand, prices will continue to be stable, or rise, so the outlook for the market in Australia is positive.

Strong demand has led to historically high rental yields, particularly in regional Australia and outer suburbs of the major capital cities. High yields mean an asset will pay for itself (i.e. it will be neutrally geared), or potentially deliver a positive cash flow income. As more investors enter the market and chase yields, these will drop as values increase (leading to capital gain profits).

You can control your property

The last benefit, and perhaps the most attractive of property investing, is control over your asset. There are very few assets other than property (or your own business) that you can buy and actively add value to. With shares and commodities you are at the mercy of the markets and/or company management to increase value.

With property investing you control your own destiny. You are not limited to the market adding value. Through education you can learn how to buy property at a great price, even in a rising market. You can source good deals and negotiate.

You can add value to your property to attract a higher rent. You can also control the costs associated with managing your property.

CHAPTER SUMMARY

To conclude this chapter, let's revisit the perceived negatives and actual positives related with investing in property. If you can think of any more negatives or positives, write them in the space at the bottom of the table.

Then try drawing a line from the perceived negative (on the left) to the corresponding actual positive on the right. For example, high entry fees are a perceived negative but this also gives the market stability, so a line can be drawn between these two. There will probably be some with multiple lines and others un-matched.

Perceived Negative	Actual Positive
Slow moving to gain capital value	Stability of market
High cost of assets	Profit comes from buying at low-market value, and value-adding
Less liquidity (takes longer to sell)	Great investments can be found when other people are scared about entering the market
Higher entry fees	Tenants pay for some utilities
Higher exit fees	Can buy positively or neutrally geared property where rent covers cost of management and maintenance
Property management fees	Insurance covers against risks
Insurance premiums	Highly automatable
Maintenance and repairs	Security
Utilities (electricity and water)	No margin calls
Managing tenants	Resilience
	Leverage
	Scalability
	Consistent performance
	High demand for property
	High rental yields
	Control over your asset
	Can actively add value
	Can source good deals even in a rising market
	Can negotiate on price

CHAPTER NOTES AND ACTIONS

Before moving on to the next chapter, spend a few minutes writing down the things that resonated with you from this chapter.

What actions do you need to take, or what do you need to plan to do, to help you get to the next level in your investing?

Write down at least 5 things now.

1. _____

2. _____

3. _____

4. _____

5. _____

3

SO WHAT'S HOLDING YOU BACK?

- *If your property investing hasn't started, or has stalled, find out why*
- *Which of the 14 common hurdles are holding you back?*
- *The following chapters will help overcome these hurdles.*

A lot of people know about all the positives of investing in property but still haven't got started. In my experience, there are 14 factors associated with property investing that can become hurdles to your investing. They will stop you from starting to invest, or, if you have bought one or two properties, they halt your progress in investing in property.

If we could, we'd all like to own a million-dollar property portfolio that pays a passive income and means we don't have to work and can instead spend our time doing whatever we want, right?

The reality is that anyone can *grow* a portfolio that could eventually reach a size that will provide a significant income stream able to fund retirement or whatever else you wish. Certainly, time may be a limiting factor which is the reason why now is as good a time to start as ever!

In this chapter, we look through the list of factors that may be holding you back from getting started in investing or growing your portfolio. You need to review the list and tick the box next to each one that applies to you.

Limiting factors preventing me from progressing in property investing include:

- ☐ I don't have enough (deposit) money to start
- ☐ I can't secure enough finance
- ☐ I don't have (free) time
- ☐ I am worried about interest rates rising
- ☐ I am worried about house prices falling
- ☐ Landlording and having tenants scares me
- ☐ I can't work out how to make money from property investing
- ☐ I don't know what kind of property to look for
- ☐ I won't know if I'm buying a lemon!
- ☐ I have or will hit a serviceability ceiling
- ☐ I don't know what structure to buy in
- ☐ I am worried about accounting, book-keeping and tax implications
- ☐ I don't know what to do to make money as a property investor
- ☐ Other _____

As you can see, common hurdles include concerns about finance, managing tenants and investment property, buying the right property that will prove profitable and coping with all the administration that goes along with investing.

Having identified the things that might be holding you back from starting, the next 14 chapters address each of them in turn and identify the solution or solutions to help you get over these hurdles so that you can move forward.

Feel free to skip the chapters that you think don't apply to you, but you may decide to read over these areas anyway – you never know what might be relevant in the future and so worth reading up on now.

I've tried to include lots of tips throughout these chapters that have worked for me and created significant profits. I've also tried to give you hints that will save you money – especially if you are starting out.

So let's get started. In the next chapter we work out how to get the deposit together.

CHAPTER SUMMARY

The next 14 chapters tackle the hurdles to property investing listed below.

- **I don't have enough (deposit) money to start** – Chapter Four looks at finding enough money to get started in your spare time.
- **I can't secure enough finance** – Chapter Five shows you how you can secure enough finance.
- **I don't have (free) time** – Chapter Six addresses finding enough time to invest.
- **I am worried about interest rates rising** – Chapter Seven covers understanding interest rates.
- **I am worried about house prices falling** – Chapters Eight and Nine explain house prices, housing markets and how to value property.
- **Landlording and having tenants, scares me** – Chapter Ten discusses property and tenant management.
- **I can't work out how to make money from property investing** – Chapter Eleven will show you how.
- **I don't know what kind of property to look for** – Chapter Twelve covers searching for and finding the right property.
- **I won't know if I'm buying a lemon!** – Chapter Thirteen explains how thorough due diligence will minimise your risk of this.
- **I have or will hit a serviceability ceiling** – Chapter Fourteen addresses servicing your debt.
- **I don't know what structure to buy in** – Chapter Fifteen explains structures you can use to maximise investment returns and protect your assets.
- **I am worried about accounting, book-keeping and tax implications** – Chapter Sixteen gives some guidelines of administration of your investments.
- **I don't know what to do to make money as a property investor** – Chapter Seventeen shares money-making techniques.

4

FINDING ENOUGH MONEY TO GET STARTED IN YOUR SPARE TIME

- *Saving and budgeting to find your deposit quicker*
- *Borrowing at a higher loan to value ratio (LVR) to get started earlier*
- *Finding a partner to invest with you*
- *Thinking more creatively.*

Not having enough money for a deposit is a very common reason for people to have difficulty starting, or progressing, in property investing. There are considerable costs involved in buying property as we have already seen.

Generally, home-loan lenders request a deposit of anything from 5% to 30% (or more), of the value of the property you would like to purchase. This means, if you are looking at a house or unit valued at $200,000 you will need a deposit of between $10,000 and $60,000. In my experience $20,000 will be around the mark. This is a reasonable sum of cash to get you going with property investing.

Additionally, because there are closing costs that are not covered by the lender, on top of the deposit you generally also need another 5% to cover stamp duty (in Australia), legal fees, pest and building inspections, etc.

That's a lot of money to start with before you even get to the property investing!

Don't despair, this hurdle can be overcome. Without sufficient deposit funds, there are several options open to you. We'll explore each of these below.

Saving and paying off debt

The simplest and easiest way to come up with deposit money, if you don't have enough, is actually to save for it. This may sound silly (for obvious reasons) but by saving money you can acquire the deposit you need without any other associated costs. Any other means of acquiring deposit money will incur a cost (whether you realise it at the time or not). For example, if you borrow the money, there will be interest to pay or you will be in someone's debt. By saving, the money belongs to you exclusively and you have complete control over it.

If you find saving difficult, then this may be a challenge. Most of us have limited income (unless we can work overtime) and there are always bills to pay and expenses coming in. If necessary, it may be prudent to find time to sit down and set a budget to track your spending and allow you to save the money you need.

If you are in debt already, then the first thing you need to do is to pay off or pay down your personal debt so that you can start saving. If you have a credit card with a $15,000 limit that is maxed out, then every year you may be paying $3,000 in interest. With these sorts of fees, saving will be even harder.

Credit cards are great things but the one rule with credit cards is that the balance on the card needs to be paid off every month – so you can get the points without paying the interest.

When I was starting out, I saved and paid down all my loans. I kept my credit card but kept the balance at zero. By paying off all my debts I was able to save much faster.

> **HOT TIP FOR INVESTORS**
>
> To start saving and paying off your credit card, adopt the following plan:
>
> 1. Write down all your expenses that occur over a month (your credit card statement may help you work this out).
> 2. Write down any annual expenses (such as car registration, insurance, etc.).
> 3. Work out your total expenses over the year and divide this by 12.
> 4. What is your annual salary, after tax? Divide this by 12.
> 5. What is the difference between #3 and #4?
>
> If #3 is bigger than #4 then you are spending more than you are earning! Work out what you can cut out, in order to reduce your spending.
>
> Aim to save at least 10% of your income.
>
> Decide how much you want to save for your first deposit (e.g. $15,000 will allow you to buy a $100,000 property plus closing costs). Based on your anticipated monthly savings, how long will it take you to reach this goal?

Negotiate a higher LVR

The second option to start investing faster is to negotiate a higher LVR.

'LVR' is a common term in property investing and stands for 'Loan to Value Ratio'. This is the proportion of the value of the property that the financier will lend, e.g. if a house is worth $500,000 and a bank will give you a $400,000 loan, then the loan to value ratio (or LVR, usually expressed as a percentage) is 80% ($400,000/$500,000).

Most banks will lend on residential property happily at 80%, leaving you to find a 20% deposit (plus costs).

If you ask your bank to lend on a higher LVR than 80%, they probably will – but there's a catch. They will more than likely ask you to pay lender's mortgage insurance (LMI). Don't be fooled, lender's mortgage insurance does nothing to protect you, it is protection for the bank, if YOU default. But they may still ask YOU to pay for it. LMI may be around 1.5% of the value of your property, depending on the LVR you are requesting. It is generally capitalised into the loan (meaning it's added onto the loan so your repayments will cover it, rather than asking you to pay it upfront). This may sound generous, but it means you pay interest on this amount over the life of the loan.

Yes, it's an additional cost of say $1,500 on a $100,000 loan, but if you are short on cash, then you might find you can buy twice as much property with a 90% LVR than an 80% LVR. If you are seeking capital gains (where the properties go up in value) then investing in two houses may well be better than investing in one, as there will be the potential to get twice the gain over the same amount of time.

Note that some lenders will offer a higher LVR (even as high as 90%) WITHOUT making you pay the lender's mortgage insurance. Visit **www.achieveproperty.com/mortgagebrokers** to find out about lenders that can give you the best deal, including perhaps, low or no LMI.

Releasing equity to fund a deposit

Equity is the difference between a property's value and the loan on it. If a house is worth $600,000 and the current loan on it is $400,000, then there is $200,000 in equity.

You can only release equity in a property that you already own, or are in the process of purchasing to fund a deposit. This property could be your own home – your principal place of residence – or it could be an investment property that you have already purchased. If you already have equity or can find it, and don't have cash, then this can be a great way to fill the gap for your next deposit.

Releasing equity in your own home

If you already own, or are in the process of purchasing your own home then you might be in a position to release equity in that property to use as a deposit for your next property purchase.

What happens here is that, if the value of your first property has increased, you can ask a bank to provide finance against the new value of the property therefore increasing your loan. These additional loan funds can provide you with a deposit on your next property. This will cost a bit more interest but will provide the deposit you need.

To make sure you have understood how this concept works, try this quiz.

> **READER QUIZ**
>
> You bought a house 10 years ago for $400,000, with an 80% LVR loan. The amount of the loan therefore was:
>
> $400,000 x 80% = _____ (a).
>
> Now the value of the property has risen to $500,000 and if a bank were to give you a loan at the same 80% LVR, they would now give you a loan of:
>
> $500,000 x 80% = _____ (b)
>
> Therefore by refinancing, the amount of equity you could release would be:
>
> (b) − (a) = _____
>
> For answers, see page 191

This may seem too simple but it is one of the easiest ways to increase your portfolio, provided you don't over-leverage (borrow too much) and you buy the right assets with the equity you release.

If you have not increased the equity in a property you own, you may be able to add some renovations which will increase its value.

Another way to raise a deposit for an investment property is to sell your own home. Your own home is not liable for capital gains tax. So these untaxed profits can go straight towards a deposit on your first investment property.

Releasing equity in your investment property

If you are in the fortunate position of already owning an investment property, with tenants paying off your mortgage, then you may be able to revalue this and increase your loan in the same way as we discussed in the previous section.

If you decide to sell your investment property to realise this profit and put it towards further investing, then you will be liable for capital gains tax.

The benefit of selling to realise a gain is that it shows on your tax return and in your book-keeping, and this makes your financial position more attractive to the banks, especially if you are on a lower income.

Using equity in an investment property you don't own YET

OK, so this one is a bit tricky, but it's really cool. It's a more advanced technique and maybe not one to start with, but still worth hearing about. You can use the equity in a property that you are in the *process of buying* to fund its deposit (instead of refinancing an existing property).

The way to do this is to use a longer settlement period and add value to the property during the settlement process. Then you get the property valued before settlement and show the bank that the value is higher than the contract price, and you want the *new value* to be used for the loan. This takes skill and negotiation but it is a great way to buy property with little money down.

The banks don't like this technique because they say "you don't have any skin in the deal" – this means that your cash exposure is reduced and they can't use your cash because you didn't give it to them. But this technique does work, and though it's harder to do post-GFC, it can definitely be done.

Finding a joint venture partner

Another means of raising capital is to partner with someone who has cash available, but not the time or inclination as you for investing. Such a partner may provide cash for a deposit for investing, or to cover closing costs, or development costs, such as for a renovation. The person providing the money is then called 'the Money Partner' and the investor managing the property deal is called 'the Time Partner'. When you partner up with someone, generally, profits and losses are split 50/50.

To make things even more fair, when the project is finished (i.e. the property has been completed and sold) and before the profits or losses are distributed, the money partner may be paid a percentage interest on the money they contributed (e.g. 7% interest per annum over the life of the project). The time partner may also be paid an amount of money that has been pre-arranged and is representative of the value of the time they spent on the project. All other costs are then deducted and any money left over is distributed 50/50.

The most important factor in any partnership is a clear understanding of the duties of each partner, and a universal goal that both partners are working towards, together. In the event that partners have different ideas on where they are heading or what each of them should be doing, the partnership is in for trouble.

A legal document which is called a Partnership Agreement should be drafted from the outset and should clearly state each of the partner's responsibilities. It will also cover what will happen in the event of a disagreement, or a loss. This document should be drafted by a solicitor. A Partnership Agreement is generally only 'needed' when there are problems or when the partnership breaks up. However, it is an invaluable tool during these situations when things go wrong and if things go smoothly, and you never need to refer to it again, even better.

A joint venture partnership is a great way for investors to get started faster and to leverage off each other's skills, finance and time.

Securing a money partner

A slightly simpler arrangement than a full joint venture is a straight money partner. This is really equivalent to a private lending arrangement. Instead of borrowing your deposit finance or development money from a traditional lender, you might borrow from a friend, colleague, family member or fellow investor.

The most important part of a money partnership is that the investor borrowing the money MUST repay the interest and/or capital WHEN they say they will.

A money partnership should also be documented by a solicitor in a specifically-drafted legal document.

Depending on the amount of money that has been funded, the money partner may request some form of security over the property or another asset. This may be in the form of a caveat (which is a registered interest on the title of the property preventing the investor selling the property until the caveat has been removed).

When an investor and money partner are starting their initial partnership, the investor might pay monthly interest, so that the money partner feels comfortable with the return they are getting (until they get to know and trust the investor fully). The rate of interest payable is dependent on the risk of the project as perceived by the money partner. As the interest rate needs to be attractive to the money partner, standard rates are usually at least a few percentage points higher than a variable home loan rate. In these circumstances, interest rates may be as high as 12% per annum, 20% per annum or even more. These additional costs need to be weighed up carefully against the opportunity to access property investing faster.

'No-money-down' deals

A no-money-down deal is a very attractive-sounding prospect to an investor without cash. Is it even possible to buy a house without using any money? It is, but it's also not as easy as it may sound. This is also a riskier strategy than simply borrowing from a traditional lender. Any investment strategy you adopt must fit your own particular risk profile.

The way that no-money-down deals are done is generally through one of two procedures – a lease option or an installment contract.

Taking up a lease option

Without going into great detail, a lease option is where the investor gains the right, but not the obligation, to buy a property. In doing so, the investor has control over the property and can then do with it what they intend in order to profit (e.g. on-sell to someone, renovate then sell, etc.). Before the property is transferred to the new buyer the option must be exercised (i.e. the property must be paid for). Using this strategy the investor can control the property with little or no money and potentially sell the property using an option, without triggering capital gains tax for themselves.

Laws surrounding property options differ depending on in which state or country the property is situated, and for more information checkout our website at **www.achieveproperty.com/vendorfinance**.

Installment contracts

An installment contract is where the property is sold to an investor who pays for it slowly over a longer period of time (in installments) rather than as a lump sum (which would require upfront finance). As the payments are smaller, the rent alone may cover the cost of repayment, or the investor may be able to fund the purchase from other cash flow, even if they wouldn't otherwise qualify for traditional finance from a standard financier. The investor may choose to rent the property that they are buying using this method, to someone else – or even to on-sell it using a similar strategy.

While both of these techniques – lease options and installment contracts – may be a great way to get started with little or no money, they may be more difficult to carry out as the other party involved may have concerns. The collective name for these techniques is 'vendor finance' and occasionally this approach gets bad press. Changes in legislation also need to be followed, and a solicitor with specific knowledge on these techniques needs to be used. However, if done right, and in the correct circumstances, these methods can provide a successful outcome for the investor.

For more details on no-money-down investing, and recommendations, check out **www.achieveproperty.com/vendorfinance**.

An easier approach to a no-money-down deal is where the investor uses some initial capital (e.g. borrows money) but then is able to quickly refinance to pay back the money, effectively doing the deal without using their own cash.

CHAPTER SUMMARY

There are many ways to find money for a deposit, even if you don't currently have the cash. The way to move forward as an investor is to be creative and discover the solutions to problems such as not having the deposit money you need. From the list below, circle the one that sounds best, and research it further (refer to Chapter Seventeen if you need places to look for more advice).

Some alternatives for finding deposit money include:

- **Save the deposit yourself** – especially when starting out, budgeting and not overspending is really important
- **Higher LVR** – shop around to find a traditional lender that will lend 90% or 95% of the purchase price, instead of 70% or 80%
- **Use equity** from refinancing for a deposit if you already have property that has gone up in value (although this will cost more in interest)
- **Create equity by adding value** and then quickly refinance to pay back your borrowings, so you don't need your own cash
- **Find a joint venture (JV) partner** who can contribute cash for a deposit while you can contribute the time managing the deal, and share the profits
- **Find a money partner** who can contribute cash for a deposit and who you pay a set interest return
- **Do a no-money-down deal** where you buy the property using a technique that allows you to control, or purchase the property without much cash

Consider carefully vendor finance opportunities.

Links

For further information related to this chapter, you can visit:

Mortgage Brokers www.achieveproperty.com/mortgagebrokers

No-Money-Down Deals www.achieveproperty.com/vendorfinance

CHAPTER NOTES AND ACTIONS

Before moving on to the next chapter, spend a few minutes writing down the things that resonated with you from this chapter.

What actions do you need to take, or what do you need to plan to do, to help you get to the next level in your investing?

Write down at least 5 things now.

1. _____

_____

_____

2. _____

_____

_____

3. _____

_____

_____

4. _____

_____

_____

5. _____

_____

_____

5

SECURING ENOUGH FINANCE

- *Why some lenders may be reluctant to give you a loan*
- *There are many different types of lenders*
- *There are three main challenges to overcome to secure finance.*

Second to not having cash for a deposit, the inability to source sufficient finance would be the most common issue faced by investors who are starting out investing in their spare time.

As a general rule, if you have a steady job, you should be able to secure finance to get started. However, there are three reasons why lenders may be reluctant to part with their money for an investor to buy property:

- Insufficient serviceability
- Perceived risk
- The deal doesn't stack up.

The good news is, you can address each of these issues and then your chances of financial success are dramatically improved! In this chapter we will work on overcoming these challenges.

But first, let's consider a few points on lending to start with.

Different types of lenders

Not all lenders are the same. In fact, mostly, lenders are very different. As an investor, one of your biggest assets (and one of the hardest things to find) is a good finance broker, because a broker will shop around many lenders and find the best one for you. There are benefits to going direct to a lender, too. Both have positives and negatives.

Borrowing through mortgage brokers

Mortgage brokers or finance brokers are people or companies whose job is to find you a lender that will provide finance for your property investing deals. As a rule, brokers will not charge you directly for their work, instead they get paid by the lender after a successful transaction has occurred. With the tightening of regulations following the global financial crisis (GFC), brokers must declare their commissions so you can see where their fees are coming from, and how much they get paid. The broker is working for you but getting paid by the banks so there may be a little bias as to which lenders are put forward to you.

The benefit of borrowing through a good finance broker is that they keep on top of changes in the banking industry and the lending criteria that banks use to determine what they will lend against. Especially when you are getting into more creative property deals and creative finance or structuring (discussed later), a good broker is essential to be able to get you the best loans at the best price for what you need.

Visit **www.achieveproperty.com/finance** for more information on finance and lending.

Borrowing directly through a bank

Dealing directly with a bank manager from one of the 'big four' (the four biggest banks in Australia – Commonwealth, Westpac, ANZ and NAB) can be a good approach to secure finance for your property investing as well. The benefit of going direct to a bank manager is that you may get better service from the bank directly, as you are dealing with one less person (i.e. there's no middleman). Bank managers also may be able to be more flexible with lending than some brokers. This is especially the case when dealing with private bankers or commercial finance, as the rules for this kind of lending are more liberal than for standard residential finance. Another benefit of commercial lending is that there is far less paperwork to fill out! (Property investors just starting out have some way to go before they are likely to be approaching a lender for commercial finance.)

The disadvantage of a direct relationship with a particular lender is that if your deal doesn't fit their criteria they aren't in a position to offer any alternatives. However, if you find a lender with whom you can deal directly, and they offer suitable terms for the deals you are doing, stick with them!

Regardless of whether you are dealing with a finance broker or a bank manager, you will need to stay in close contact and follow up with them regularly to ensure that your loan progresses as quickly as you need. Have your contact provide a timeline of milestones. For example:

- What date they expect unconditional approval
- When the bank's valuation will be back
- When unconditional approval is due.

Follow up to see that these milestones are met (although it's realistic to expect some delays) but keep on top otherwise timelines may blow out substantially.

Three challenges to securing a loan

So, let's look in more detail at the three reasons that lenders may have difficulty financing an investor or a project.

Securing enough finance

Insufficient serviceability

Serviceability is the ability for the borrower (you) to service the loan – that is, whether you are able to make the repayments on the loan. When a lender is assessing your ability to repay a loan (or at least the interest, if it is an interest-only loan) they will consider various things:

- The potential income that can be generated by the property you are purchasing (assuming it is an investment property). As a rule, the higher the rent possible, the better.
- The debt carried by the borrower, as this will impede serviceability of the home loan. Having to simultaneously be paying off personal debt, such as car loans, credit cards, store cards, etc., will reduce your ability to pay off a loan on investment property, as you may be overcommitted.
- Your personal income will play a big role in determining your ability to service the loan. If you are self-employed, financiers may see this as more of a risk than if you are an employee (i.e. paying monthly pay as you go (PAYG) tax). They may discount your income when they assess it.

> **HOT TIP FOR INVESTORS**
> Always ask the real estate agency to provide a written letter advising the market rent of a property you are intending to purchase as this can be used when submitting your application for finance. It is better if the selling agent is not the person who gives the rental appraisal.

- Any children or dependants you may have will reduce your serviceability (as the financier feels that you will need to spend money on them). Having to pay child support will do the same.

- Other income that you have coming in (e.g. from other businesses or other investment properties) will help improve your serviceability.
- Interest rates – financiers will base their assessments on interest rates higher than the current rate, so as to allow for interest rate fluctuations in the future. Obviously, the higher the interest rate, the more interest you need to pay, and this will affect your ability to borrow.

If you want to assess your ability to service property that you are looking at buying, your finance broker may be able to give you a serviceability calculator that helps you estimate how much lending you could access, depending on different conditions.

In the event that you are told that you cannot service a loan, it will be for one of these reasons above.

For some investors who have already started buying property, they might hit a 'serviceability ceiling' whereby, based on the income they receive from their job and other property, they have already purchased all the real estate they can for the time being at the current yield that it is renting for. That is, based on the rent being generated, unless they can buy property that is substantially more cash flow positive, they are limited by their ability to safely pay the interest when it is due, so they can't borrow any more.

The only options, when you reach your serviceability ceiling are to:

- Wait until your property starts generating more income (rent goes up but expenses stay the same, or go down)
- Sell down some less-performing properties to pay down debt
- Find a way to increase your income (get a new job, another business, or develop your properties to increase their yield).

If you can find a way to increase your cash flow, then your serviceability will improve.

Perceived risk

It may be that you can actually service a loan but a financier still won't lend you all the money you need because they perceive you or your deal to be too great a risk. In this case, often a lender will give you funds but will reduce the LVR they allow to cover themselves in the event of default.

Depending on the kind of finance you are seeking, a bank's risk profile will differ. Residential finance is generally seen as less risky than commercial finance as, in general, people need houses and the housing market overall is fairly stable. Commercial finance is seen as more risky, therefore LVRs are generally lower.

When assessing risk, lenders will consider your risk as the borrower and the property you intend buying that will secure the loan. The list below is not exhaustive but includes what will generally be assessed by a lender:

- **Age** – are you too young and inexperienced or too old and unable to keep working to pay back your loan?
- **Employment** – if you have not been in your job for very long, especially if you are still in a probationary period, this is perceived as risky as there is a chance that you may lose your job.
- **Time you have lived at your current address** – lenders like to know they will be able to find you if they need to, and confirm who you are. If you haven't lived in your house for long they will want other previous addresses to cross-reference. If you have been continually moving from place to place, alarm bells may start to ring.

- **Occupation** – a professional such as a doctor, lawyer or accountant will be seen as a lower risk than a blue-collar worker, and may attract better finance packages.
- **The location of the property** – some postcodes are seen as a higher risk for default and may be harder to borrow against.
- **The type of property and oversupply** – some inner city apartments are seen as risky due to oversupply and may not be lent against or may have lower LVRs.

The best person to speak to about all of the above is your finance broker when considering your risk profile or the riskiness of finance for a particular property you are looking to purchase. A good finance broker will be able to provide instruction on how best to fill in finance applications that will give you the best chance of approval.

One important tip when filling in a finance application is to be thorough and get it right the first time. If you leave blanks on the form your application may get partly processed then sent to the bottom of the pile. When you are wanting fast approval the best thing you can do is to fill in the form completely and provide ALL the necessary supporting documentation. No one enjoys filling out finance applications, but it is an important part of being an investor!

The deal doesn't stack up

There is a rule in property investing, "If the deal is good enough, you will always find finance for it". The same goes in reverse – if you can't finance a deal, it may be that the deal doesn't stack up. We will go into more detail later regarding what makes for a good deal, but if there is insufficient equity and/or yield from a property, or if the property you are purchasing is coming back with a low valuation, then you may find that lenders just won't finance it – for good reason! It may just be a dud.

Part of your due diligence is to ensure that a property you buy is worth what you pay for it and that it can be financed. In some cases, an undeveloped property may be worth less than you pay for it, because the vendor knows that after development the value will be significantly increased. For these deals you might need to accept a lower LVR and use more cash or other borrowings initially.

What to do when you cannot get enough finance

You have several options when you can't get enough finance from a lender. The first thing to do is find out from your broker or bank why they won't lend you the finance. Ensure that the reason is not that the deal doesn't stack up. If the property you are considering really does offer great cash flow and has good capital gains potential then keep searching and you will find finance somewhere.

Also, ensure that your application has not been rejected due to circumstances that have changed or that you can change. For example, you may have secured a second job, had a pay-rise or passed your probationary period at work.

When you can't get finance and are considering your options, here's what you can do. You will recognise some of these strategies from the previous chapter.

Use more cash or equity, if you have it

If you are being refused finance, you might be able to approach a lender for a lower LVR loan, and if you can buy using some more cash of your own then often this is the easiest way. Later you can then re-value and re-finance the property after you have purchased, to free up your cash again. This may be a very successful way to quickly grow your equity, if you can buy property below value and then refinance after a renovation, or value-add.

Find a partner

Your second option, if you don't have cash or equity, is to seek out a money partner or joint venture partner as discussed previously.

Vendor finance

Another option is vendor finance (but you must consider the additional risks and complexities associated with this strategy).

An effective creative strategy can be to use vendor finance with the vendor 'carrying back' some of the cost of the property which you agree to pay at a later date. If your plan is to renovate or develop the property and you know that you will be able to sell or refinance to release some capital when you have finished, then the vendor may agree to you paying an amount (maybe 20%) later, and this could help resolve your finance 'gap'.

Securing a second mortgage

Lastly, you might be able to secure a second mortgage. In this situation, you will have a first mortgage from a traditional lender and another mortgage from a different lender (for the amount that the first lender would not lend). Both lenders need to know about the other, but this can be a way to get extra lending if you are knocked back. Rest assured that the second mortgage will be at a higher interest rate than the first. This is because the risk for the second mortgagee is higher. If you default on the property, the first mortgagee gets paid out first and there may be nothing left to pay back the second loan.

CHAPTER SUMMARY

If you can't get a bank to finance a property deal, it is likely it will be for one of the following reasons:

- **Insufficient serviceability** – the bank doesn't think you have enough money coming in to comfortably pay the interest on the loan.
- **Perceived risk** – the bank is worried that you might default.
- **The deal doesn't stack up** – there is not enough cash flow from the property, or not enough capital (equity) or the property has been over-valued.

If you aren't having success getting finance then find out from your broker the reason why. If you can overcome their reasons for not financing the deal then they may come to the party.

Other options for finding finance solutions include:

- Using more cash/equity then refinancing after adding value
- Using a money partner or JV partner
- Using vendor finance or taking out a second mortgage.

If a deal is really good, there will be a way to find the finance needed to make it work.

Links

For further information related to this chapter, you can visit:

Finance and Lending
www.achieveproperty.com/finance.

CHAPTER NOTES AND ACTIONS

Before moving on to the next chapter, spend a few minutes writing down the things that resonated with you from this chapter.

What actions do you need to take, or what do you need to plan to do, to help you get to the next level in your investing?

Write down at least 5 things now.

1. _____
   _____
   _____

2. _____
   _____
   _____

3. _____
   _____
   _____

4. _____
   _____
   _____

5. _____
   _____
   _____

6

FINDING ENOUGH TIME TO INVEST

- *It's more about making time than finding time*
- *Identify the real reason you want to start investing in property*
- *Learn better time management strategies.*

Everyone wishes they had more time to do the things they want to do. For many people, investing is something that they would love to do "if only I had the time…" This book is here to convince you that you can become a successful property investor in your spare time. My experience has proved that this is possible. The important thing is to make sure that you use your spare time wisely.

We live in a busy world and seem to spend so much time doing things for other people – our boss, our friends, family, children, pets…

If this sounds like you then this is an important chapter for you to read. Make sure you find the time to do so!

Finding focus

There is one truth about lack of time and that is that people who don't *have* time to do something either don't really *want* to do it or aren't *focused* on the task.

If something is important enough, you will find time to do it. If you can't find the time, then really, something else *was* more important. So the real truth is, if you can't find time to invest, because you have to look after your kids, for example, then either:

- You would *rather* be looking after your children than investing for your future and their future
- You are too busy looking after your children to focus on what may be more important in the long run, which is figuring out how to have your children cared for WHILE you invest for your future and their future

Finding your reason to find time

One of the reasons that people don't want to do something (and I mean REALLY WANT to do something, e.g. the I-will-stop-at-nothing-until-I-complete-this-goal kind of wanting) is because they lack a REASON to achieve it. This book is focused on getting started in investing, so we are not going to go into great detail on success mindset (let's save that for the next book), but if you are struggling to find time, even though you really want to invest, then perhaps you haven't yet figured out your REASON for investing.

There are many reasons for investing and none of them are "I just want to be rich".

Everyone has something, or several things that drive them – their love of family, a vision of a better world, fast cars, charities, lifestyle, fame, a love of travel… These are all things that can be better achieved by being financially free or at least financially better off. If you can find your "dream" (your REASON for investing), and use this as motivation when things get hard, then you have a much better chance of success.

So, if you are failing to find time to get started on your investing, think about your REASON, and if you don't start taking action, how it will feel to never achieve your goal. Then figure out a way to find the time you need to start heading closer to that dream.

Time management

To motivate ourselves we just need a strategy. We know we want to spend time on investing but how do we deal with the things that seem to want to use up our time, all the time?

There are a range of good books on time management. For further advice on this topic, if you need it, check out **www.achieveproperty.com/timemanagement**.

In the meantime (no pun intended) here are a few things you can do to try and find more time in the day for things that are important:

Covey's quadrant

Stephen R. Covey* devised a means of sorting tasks into urgency and importance, in what became known as Covey's quadrant.

1 Urgent and Important	2 Important but Not Urgent
3 Urgent but Not Important	4 Not Urgent nor Important

*Covey is author of *The Seven Habits of Highly Effective People*, one of the highest-bestselling business and self-help books published of all time

Tasks that fit into quadrant #1 are emergencies – things that need to be done right away, and are really important. These are things on deadlines and things that will be disastrous if not done now. People who live in quadrant #1 are stressed and, while they may be productive, they often burn out.

The recommendation is to try and keep as many of your tasks as you can in quadrant #2. This means addressing tasks that are important BEFORE they become urgent. This may mean resourcing sufficiently so that you can dedicate the time to getting things finished ahead of deadlines, rather than on deadlines.

Tasks that are Urgent but Not Important should be delegated to someone else. After all, if they are not important for you to do, why do them yourself when you could be doing something better?

Tasks that are Not Urgent nor Important should be left undone.

How many things are you doing that are neither urgent nor important, but are taking up time that could be re-prioritised for investing? Are you living in quadrant #1, and what are you going to do about it?

Learning to prioritise

To really get a grip on time management, ask yourself some questions:

- **What is the thing that will make me the most money today?** When trying to decide the order of tasks to do, good time management will prevail if you prioritise based on value. As an investor, or a business-owner, one of our focuses needs to be commercial, so sometimes a useful criterion in determining what to prioritise is simply on the basis of financial return. If you spend your time on things that AREN'T going to make money, where will you end up?
- **Mastery over procrastination – do it now!** Procrastination is an interesting human behaviour. For various reasons, if we are uncomfortable or unprepared for something we avoid it. One of the secrets to success is to tackle

procrastination head-on. If tasks seem daunting, we should throw ourselves into them, endeavouring to get them finished as quickly as we can in order to move onto the next item. Not only will this stop us from wasting time (doing things that are unproductive in an attempt to justify the avoidance of another task), it will help us quickly achieve the important goals that we set, so that we can move onto the next ones.

- **Don't allow distractions.** Distractions such as email, telephones, Facebook, and (some) people, can be great time-wasters and can result in significantly reduced productivity. If you don't have time for investing, how much time do you spend on any of the above? Could you find another 20 minutes a day (or a lot more) by reducing one of these distractions?

  If you find that it is impossible to stop these things from distracting you, consider turning off your smart-phone (this may eliminate both the telephone and Facebook distractions), only open your email program twice a day, and put up a sign on your door that says: Do Not Disturb.

  You will get a lot more work done by avoiding distractions and in your spare time you can dedicate some more time to investing instead.

- **Television.** One of the greatest time-wasters of the modern world is television. While it is great to be able to relax and watch TV with friends, or after a hard day's work, how much time do you spend every week watching TV and how is this really contributing to your life? If you cut out just two TV shows a week and instead spent the time on investing, what difference might this make in a year?

- **Plan for success.** Do you schedule time for investing? Do you have a diary or smart-phone with a calendar function that you can use to block off time for a purpose such as investing? If you are finding that there are things that you want to get done, but can't find the time, set an appointment ahead in your calendar for the next day or week, and when it comes around, you have made time for the task.

  One of the best ways to do this is to dedicate one day a week to setting your tasks for the upcoming week. The more specific you are with your tasks and setting when you will achieve them, the more efficient you will be and the more likely you will achieve all your goals.

- **Start early or finish later.** If you are finding that your 'day job' doesn't leave time for investing, try starting the day an hour earlier or finishing it an hour later. You can fit in investing time before or after work and, most likely, people won't miss you if you start or finish early or late.

- **Delegate or outsource.** As there are so many things in life that are time-intensive, most of us don't finish everything we want to do in a day – whether at work, or in our home and family lives. And there are some things that, no matter how hard we try to do quickly, take a long time and offer little reward (ironing and cleaning come to mind for me).

  While most of us also don't have unlimited sources of income, it may be more efficient to pay for someone else to do something that they can do faster, for a small price, allowing us to focus on a task that we can do which will earn us more money, or bring us a step closer to financial freedom. The power of delegation and outsourcing is unlimited and should not be overlooked when trying to free up time. For ideas or inspirations on outsourcing, check out **www.achieveproperty.com/outsourcing**.

- **Take time off.** Lastly, if you work a busy 9 to 5 job (or 8 to 7), 5 days a week (or more) and the weekends are spent with family and you are struggling to find time to start investing for your future, you sound like you need a holiday.

    Consider taking annual leave (either one day at a time, or a small block) to allow you to at least start planning, or to free up time to do one of your Urgent and Important tasks that will set you on the course towards financial freedom. I have known people to take one day of annual leave each week for half a year – effectively dropping down to four days a week which makes a significant difference to their ability to reach their goal of financial freedom.

    The reality is that working towards financial freedom takes time, and you have to find this time to be able to reach your goal. Trying to just work harder may work in the short term but financial freedom, like any worthy ideal, won't be achieved in just the short term.

The next step then is perhaps to negotiate with your work to reduce your time at work to four days instead of five. If you are serious about financial freedom then this may be a necessary progression – and like everything, it will come at a cost. The questions you need to address are: What will it take for you to achieve your financial freedom? What will the cost be? Are you prepared to do it?

CHAPTER SUMMARY

- If someone says they don't have time to do something, generally they either don't really want to do it or aren't focused on the task. If you find yourself saying this (to yourself, or to others), think about which it is and decide what you need to do differently.

- Everyone needs to find his or her 'reason' to find time to invest – this will give them the motivation to get the work done.

- Use Covey's quadrant to sort through the items on your list – prioritise and do the most important first. Delegate the Urgent but Not Important tasks, and delete the tasks that aren't important or urgent.

- Tackle procrastination head on. If there is something that you find yourself procrastinating over, either (a) just do it now or (b) schedule time when you know you will be available and do it then. Either way ensure you get it done.

- Don't allow distractions. If you find yourself getting distracted about a task, eliminate the distraction (move yourself, or switch off the device causing the problem), or re-schedule to complete the task when you won't be distracted.

- Plan for success! Seriously. Do it now.

Links

Here are links to more time management books and techniques
www.achieveproperty.com/timemanagement

Ideas and inspirations on outsourcing
www.achieveproperty.com/outsourcing

Finding enough time to invest

CHAPTER NOTES AND ACTIONS

Before moving on to the next chapter, spend a few minutes writing down the things that resonated with you from this chapter.

What actions do you need to take, or what do you need to plan to do, to help you get to the next level in your investing?

Write down at least 5 things now.

1. _____

2. _____

3. _____

4. _____

5. _____

7

UNDERSTANDING INTEREST RATES

- *There are two interest rates quoted in the media*
- *Historical interest rates provide a benchmark for future interest rates*
- *Property investors should calculate their potential cash flow, taking into account possible interest rate rises.*

Interest rate fears – especially as interest rates are rising – are a leading reason for first-time investors to hold off purchasing property. When you have not been in the property market before, you don't have a feel of how the market moves or how external forces, such as interest rates, may affect the value of your investment, or your ability to make your mortgage repayments. In this chapter, we will look at some factors around interest rates to help provide a realistic perspective on what impact rates may have on our investing.

Interest rates affect more than just property investors

Firstly, what are interest rates and why are they here? There are two kinds of interest rates to be aware of:

- **Standard variable** interest rate set by each of the banks and lending institutions
- **Cash rate** set by the Reserve Bank of Australia (RBA).

As property investors, we are really interested in the standard variable rates as these determine how much interest we pay on our borrowings. These rates, as I mentioned earlier, are controlled by each bank. However, the cash rate influences the standard variable rates of the banks.

Cash rates and the RBA

Interest rate rises and falls are measured in basis points which are degrees of a percentage point. 25 basis points equals a quarter of a percent, and mostly interest rates will drop or increase by a quarter or maybe half a percent at most.

The only time we see more drastic movement in interest rates is when something major is happening to the economy and a sudden correction is needed. This happened during the global financial crisis when the RBA cut its interest rates by 100 basis points (a full 1%) in October 2008; then by 75 basis points (0.75%) in November 2008; 100 basis points (1%) in December 2008; and another 100 basis points (1%) in February 2009. That's an almost unprecedented 3.75% in under a year and a half. These dramatic cuts were made in an effort to keep Australia out of recession.

Normally, the RBA is more cautious when it makes changes to the cash rate. Adjustments are usually 0.25%, or 25 basis points, at a time.

The official cash rate

So where does the cash rate fit in? The Reserve Bank sets what is called the official cash rate (OCR), this is a rate at which banks lend or borrow money between themselves on the overnight money markets. This cost then influences the cost of borrowing, which impacts on the cost of lending to consumers and businesses.

As a rule, when the official cash rate goes up, banks will

increase their standard variable rates, and similarly when the cash rate goes down so do banks' lending interest rates.

The reason the RBA makes changes to the official cash rate is to stimulate or contract borrowing and spending, to keep inflation across the whole economy within a predetermined limit. While this affects property investors' mortgage interest repayments, it also affects the interest payments for anyone who has debt (including home-owners, businesses, etc.). In Australia, the Reserve Bank meets on the first Tuesday of every month and at their board meeting, they discuss and set the new cash rate for that month if they think a change is necessary.

Supply and demand

However, what really influences the standard variable interest rates charged by the banks is supply and demand. The cash rate influences the supply side of the equation because the higher the cash rate, the more expensive money borrowing becomes (therefore supply of cheaper money is reduced). At the same time, the more that banks want to *lend* money (supply increases), the more competitive their rates will be, and the more that consumers and businesses want to borrow (demand increases), the more banks will be able to charge. Luckily, there is usually an equilibrium in that when people want to borrow the banks also want to lend, so rates generally stay in a relatively tight range.

What has been seen during the GFC is that the Reserve Bank has dropped rates to help stimulate the economy but the banks have not passed on the full rate drop to consumers. As an investor, there is no point getting too hung up on this. As the economy improves and competition between banks increases, rates will become more competitive again. In the meantime, let's focus on the great property deals that are around.

Interest rates are outside of your control

The take-home message about interest rates is that while they may have a significant impact on the amount of interest that property investors pay, they are a factor out of an investor's control. You need to know about interest rates but not worry over them.

It is helpful to understand the historical range that interest rates have moved in. This will give you an idea of what is likely, or at least possible, to occur in the future.

Figure 7.1 shows interest rates for the 20 years from August 1992 to August 2012. This graph demonstrates that for the last 20 years, the cash rate has stayed between 3% and 8%.

Figure 7.1 – RBA cash rate percentage, August 1992 – August 2012

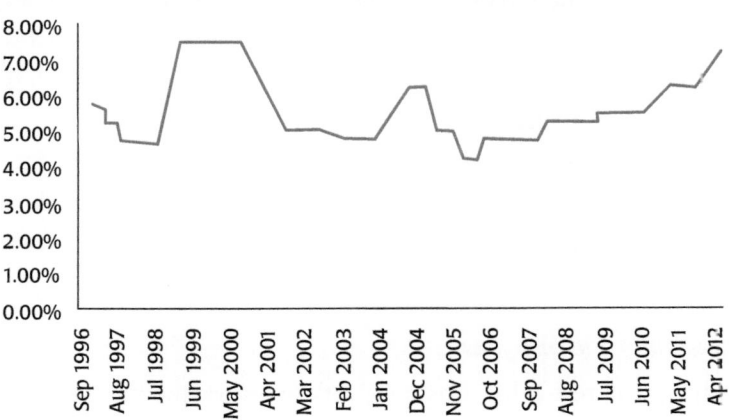

Source: RBA http://www.rba.gov.au/statistics/tables/index.html#interest_rates

Standard residential variable interest rates, as set by the banks, are generally 2% to 3% higher at most. It is safe to assume that, unless there is a significant change to the economy, this is a safe range to make our projections for interest rates when we calculate the likely interest rate movements into the foreseeable future.

The impact of interest rate changes

Having looked at the likely range for interest rates into the future, the second thing to consider is the impact of interest rate changes on our investing, including our ability to service any loans we have taken out or are considering taking out.

Back in 2008, just before the GFC hit, the cash rate and standard variable interest rates were approaching a 20-year high in Australia. In May 2008, the cash rate was 7.25%, a rate which hadn't been seen since January in 1995, 13 years earlier. Understandably, some borrowers were getting concerned. The media was suggesting that rates might keep climbing higher to record levels not seen since the boom and bust of the 1980s. So some borrowers decided they should fix their loans at the then current (high) rates, instead of risking that rates would move higher still. Months later, rates fell to record lows and these borrowers paid significant penalties to change their loans.

We are not going to go into the pros and cons of fixed versus variable interest rate loans here, however, what is worth considering is what effect interest rates and interest payments have on your investing.

Interest rates and cash flow

Mortgage interest is for most property investors the most significant cost to their property investment portfolios. When considering the risk of interest rate rises, we need to look at the impact of mortgage interest on our cash flow.

Cash flow is the money moving into and out from our businesses or investments. An understanding of cash flow is imperative to the success of a business person or investor. People and businesses don't commonly go bankrupt because of their assets dropping in value. However, they do go bankrupt quickly and commonly due to an inability to pay their debtors, because their flow of cash (cash flow) has stopped.

When we have a healthy business, we have more money (revenue) coming in, and less money (expenses) moving out. We can pay our staff, our running costs, and any other incidentals and everyone is happy. On top of this, we are able to make a profit which we can re-invest to grow the business or put in our pocket!

However, if our revenue drops, or if our expenses increase to the point that we are paying more money out than we have coming in, this is when we get into trouble. Our cash flow in these circumstances is reduced and may even be negative. We stop generating profit and may need to borrow to pay our expenses. It may be necessary to sell assets in order to pay our bills. If our cash flow is negative for too long, and we run out of assets to sell but still have bills to pay, we become insolvent.

The risk for investors from interest rates, therefore, lies at the point that interest rates might reach, where our total income is exceeded by our total expenses and our cash flow becomes negative.

As educated investors, we need to decide how much we can borrow, at current interest rates, given the income that our investments will generate.

Our degree of risk tolerance will determine the 'buffer' we are happy with. It will take into account that interest rates might rise or fall over the time period we intend to hold the asset, based on historical trends. By assessing this logically we can overcome the fear of interest rises and make an educated decision regarding the degree of risk that we are happy to take, in order to start investing for our future.

As an exercise, consider the quiz below.

READER QUIZ

Current cash rate	3% (this is historically low)
Current bank interest rate	6%
Rental yield	10%
Cost to buy investment	$100,000
Borrowing percentage (LVR)	80%
Interest cost (per annum)	$_____
Maintenance cost (per annum)	$_____
	(assume 4% of purchase cost)
Rental income (per annum)	$_____
Cash flow (per annum)	$_____
With a possible rise in rates of	4% (conservatively high)
New interest cost (per annum)	$_____
Maintenance cost (per annum)	$_____
	(assume 4% of purchase cost)
Rental income (per annum)	$_____
New cash flow (per annum)	$_____

For answers, see page 191

Based on these calculations, in the event that interest rates rose by 4% (which is a significantly high increase) to 10% p.a., and assuming that nothing else changed (e.g. rental income didn't rise to offset the increase), how much out of pocket, over a year, would you be?

This would be a worst-case scenario but if it happened and you had bought an investment such as this would you be in a position to find the shortfall somewhere – perhaps from your salary or savings – to get through this period?

Interest rate fluctuations are a normal part of the market. The job of the investor is to ensure that their investing business can tolerate these fluctuations.

The benefit of having an investing model that can withstand

Understanding interest rates

these market forces is that your potential for better capital gains is increased. This is because you will be able to buy when others are scared off by interest rates or poor market sentiment which means you can buy at a better price.

Next we will look at the potential for capital gains with fluctuations in the housing market.

CHAPTER SUMMARY
- Interest rate movements affect the cost of money for banks and borrowers.
- Investors are affected as interest rate rises reduce cash flow.
- Cash flow is the amount of money coming in to the investor. It consists of income (rent), less all expenses (mortgage interest, rates, insurance, property maintenance and management, etc.). The better the cash flow of the portfolio, the easier an investor can service more debt.
- Interest payable on a mortgage is generally one of the highest costs to the investor, and one of the most variable expenses (depending on interest rates fluctuations).
- Interest rate movements affect an investor's ability to service more debt.
- While investors can fix interest rates, banks generally charge penalties for paying down debt (e.g. selling) during the fixed period, or remortgaging to get out of this arrangement. So investors should be careful about fixing rates.
- Investors should create a property portfolio that is able to adequately and comfortably service the debt (mortgage) that they intend to take on. They should calculate an interest rate buffer to make sure they can withstand any likely rises.
- A good investing model will allow the investor to withstand interest rate rises over the term they are looking to hold their assets.

CHAPTER NOTES AND ACTIONS

Before moving on to the next chapter, spend a few minutes writing down the things that resonated with you from this chapter.

What actions do you need to take, or what do you need to plan to do, to help you get to the next level in your investing?

Write down at least 5 things now.

1. _____

2. _____

3. _____

4. _____

5. _____

8

HOUSE PRICES AND HOUSING MARKETS

- *House prices are driven by supply and demand*
- *The supply of money contributes to buyers' ability to purchase property*
- *Government and economic factors influence demand*
- *There is not one property market in Australia, but multiple sub-markets*
- *It is important to be able to understand price data and recognise trends.*

We hear about house prices pretty regularly in the media. When the property market is moving positively, we are told that we need to buy or miss out on the boom. When the market is going sideways (i.e. prices are staying the same) or even trending slightly down, we are told that prices will plummet, "like they did in the US during the GFC", and that anyone who owns property will lose substantial amounts of money.

To substantiate these emotive claims, all sorts of statistics and expert witnesses are called upon.

In some cases, the same newspaper will run two opposing articles in the same edition. Or sometimes the stories of one day are totally discredited the following day. These sorts of media reports are not only commonplace, they are often not based on any real credible evidence, only opinion.

No wonder it is hard to make a rational conclusion, when

starting to invest in property, as to how the property market is likely to perform with respect to house prices.

There's no crystal ball

Now, before we go any further in this chapter, let's be clear – no one can see the future and we don't *know* what house prices are going to do. However, we can make rational observations of where prices are at and the possible or likely movement of prices, based on market conditions and the market forces at play.

The reality is that house prices, like all prices, are dictated by the fundamentals of supply and demand. Furthermore, house price movements follow the supply of money that is used to buy the houses.

Understanding these two fundamental principles gives us a better understanding of why prices move the way they do. It also permits us to assess the likelihood (or not) of severe price crashes, as were seen in some areas of the US housing market during the early stages of the GFC.

Housing supply and demand in a nutshell

Entire volumes have been written on housing supply and demand. Governments and developers spend millions of dollars working out models to predict market needs and forecast growth trends and the population's housing requirements for the future. As an investor, we need to know what may influence supply and demand in the areas we are considering investing, as this may reflect future capital appreciation or depreciation.

In Australia, the supply of property in general is quite restricted (although you may find local oversupply in some areas, for example as has occurred in the past in the Melbourne city residential apartment market and in accommodation on the Gold Coast). Overall, Australia is said to currently have a housing supply shortage, which is reflected by generally low rental vacancy rates.

As for demand for real estate, this comes from two areas – principally the home-owner market and the property investment market. The demand for properties by home-owners is influenced by varying forces, but in particular:

- People's ability to source finance
- The cost of buying versus renting
- Market sentiment (whether people think that buying now is a good idea or not).

Market sentiment can be self-fulfilling, when people think that prices will go up and that buying is a good idea, more people buy which drives prices higher. Similarly when people think that prices won't rise, they stop buying, which reduces price increases.

The demand for property by investors is driven by two potential profit outcomes:

- Rental yield
- Capital gain potential.

If investors can see that property is likely to go up in value, then there may be an increased demand from investors wishing to buy before prices increase (then sell when prices are higher, to make a profit). This too can then be a self-fulfilling prophecy as investor demand itself drives prices to start with.

Follow the money

House price movements follow the supply of money that is buying the houses. In both the investor and home-owner markets, one of the key forces that drives price is the supply of money used to buy the asset.

Most people would rather own their home than rent (so long as they can afford it). And the majority of people also don't have the cash to buy a house outright so they are dependent on bank finance for purchasing.

For property investors, leverage (borrowing) is almost always used so, again, bank finance is necessary for these buyers.

A home-owner's ability to finance buying a house depends on two factors:

- How much deposit they have saved (or how much they need for a deposit);
- How high interest rates are (therefore how much interest repayments are going to cost them).

Banks then dictate the terms that influence home-buyers' ability to enter the housing market. They can do so by increasing or decreasing the percentage of deposit needed and by increasing or decreasing interest rates.

So, as an example, if a bank is willing to lend 90% of the value of a house at an interest rate of 5%, then a home-buyer will only need 10% deposit and interest is relatively cheap. This will make it easier to buy a house than if the bank is asking for a 20% deposit and if interest rates were at 7%.

When the deposit required by banks decreases and when interest rates also decrease then more people are able to access money to buy houses, therefore this will lift demand – and so prices will go… up.

Government influences on property prices

Government incentives, designed to stimulate buying in certain sectors of the property market, will also have an impact on buyers' ability to purchase property. The First Home Owners Grant (FHOG) is a state-based initiative and currently most states only offer the FHOG to home-buyers purchasing new properties (check your state government's websites for more details).

An increase in the FHOG may mean that first-time buyers have access to more deposit money, making it easier for them to buy. Stamp duty concessions may also reduce the amount of cash needed, making buying easier. Both of these scenarios will help first-time buyers purchase a property but will also help increase prices in this section of the market as demand is increased.

When it comes to investors, they may use equity and other people's money instead of cash for deposits, so they may be less affected by deposit requirements than home-owners. For this reason, the property market driven by investors may move separately to the market driven by home-owners.

Employment levels

When people are earning more money (and can therefore afford to pay more interest) then it will be easier for them to buy houses and demand for houses will go up. When unemployment is low, and when wages are growing, this generally has a positive effect on property prices. Increases can occur nationally (during good economic times), or regionally (where specific areas see jobs growth, usually from local infrastructure, developments, mining, etc.).

Future supply and demand

One thing to look out for, when assessing the future for potential shifts in the property market, is a sudden change that may affect the supply of money into the property market or an increase in demand for properties on a larger scale.

Changes in money supply in the past have been seen when increased flexibility in lending in Australia led to the property boom of the 1990s and early 2000s. The introduction of the FHOG in the early 2000s, to offset the introduction of the GST, also helped fuel the property boom that ensued. (The GST was a Goods and Services Tax of 10% introduced by the Howard Government in Australia in 2000.)

Increase in SMSF borrowings

As we look to the future, factors that could trigger the next property boom could include a re-introduction of a FHOG across all property – not just on new property – (which will increase first home-buyer demand), and increased lending to self managed superannuation funds (SMSFs) which until recently were not able to use leverage to buy property.

As borrowing in superannuation becomes more popular and commonplace, a large amount of money could enter the property market, especially following the losses and poor performance of the sharemarkets during the GFC. Should this occur, we may see further rises in the Australia property market in the near future.

Locating areas to buy

The take-home message here is if you are trying to locate areas where prices might move higher, look at the supply of money that would be funding buying. If supply is likely to increase, then so too may demand, resulting in an increase in prices in the future.

Figure 8.1 below demonstrates the growth of property prices, and the volume of property sales, in the town of Quirindi, where I bought my first-ever investment property back in 2004.

House prices and housing markets

Figure 8.1 – Quirindi sales and growth

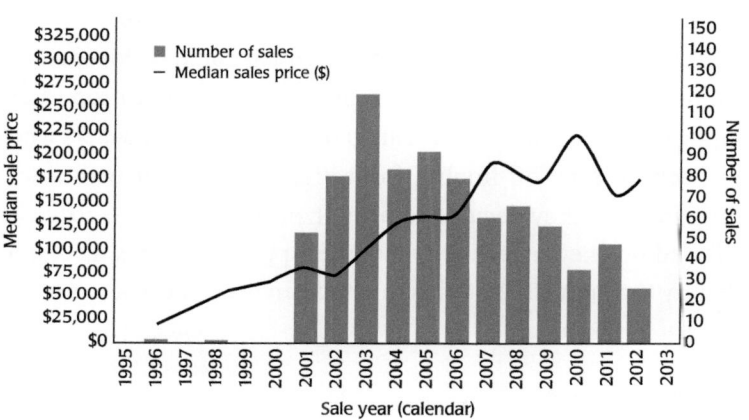

© Pricefinder 2012, reprinted with permission

The vertical bars represent the number of sales per year (right-hand y-axis) and the line running across the graph represents the median house price (left-hand y-axis). What we can see here is that there was a high volume of sales from 2001 to 2009 that started declining slightly from around 2007. In 2011, median sales dropped significantly, though the volume of sales increased slightly on 2010.

What this graph shows to me is, that from 1996 through to 2010, price growth was on the rise (including when I bought back in 2004). This was fuelled by the availability of money to the people who were interested in buying. In many cases these people were investors like myself, but also home-owners in the town who could afford a house and wanted to buy.

It is interesting to note, that at the height of the GFC (from 2008 to 2010) house prices continued to climb. This reflects that even though banks were getting tighter on lending, the affordability of houses in the $150,000 to $225,000 range meant that

GFC conditions did not affect this property market, compared to some other markets that saw declines in price as a result.

2011 saw a decline in median price which could be for various reasons. Reasons might include: a number of cheaper properties coming on to the market and selling; or discounting by sellers who had been holding off hoping for a higher price, but with sales falling in 2010, they decided to drop their price to sell in 2011.

Based on the current graph, prices appear to be rising again half-way through 2012, so this might be an indication of a market recovery in this area.

Median sale prices

It is worth briefly commenting on the median sale price, as this is the price reported in all property data. The median is the 'middle' price, not the average. See below for a quick explanation of median, as this can be misleading.

Here are seven example sales in a region, over the course of a year:

20-Jan	$100,000
13-Mar	$120,000
17-Jul	$50,000
20-Aug	$20,000
1-Oct	$90,000
12-Nov	$100,000
15-Nov	$110,000

Without looking at the answers below, take a guess at what the MEDIAN and MEAN price is for this period for this region.

OK – here are the answers.

The Median price is $100,000.
The Mean price (average) is $84,286.

Which price is more important to an investor? And why are these numbers different? The reality is that both are important for different reasons and both can be misleading if interpreted incorrectly.

The median price is the middle number in the dataset. Where there is a large quantity of data, this can be a quite useful figure, especially if you are looking at buying or selling around this price.

If we sort the data from low to high, we can identify the median price fairly easily:

$20,000
$50,000
$90,000
$100,000
$100,000
$110,000
$120,000

The mean price is a number that generally isn't reported, but people often think the median is a mean (a different kind of average). The mean would be the average price, calculated by combining all the sale prices and dividing by the total number of sales, e.g. $20,000 + $50,000 + $90,000 + $100,000 + $100,000 + $110,000 + $120,000, divided by 7 sales = $84,286.

The mean is more useful when we don't have significant outliers (extraordinary sale prices – either at the top or bottom end of the market), as this could represent a likely price you might get for a given sale.

In both cases, extreme high or low sales can skew the data, and this needs to be taken into consideration. Also, a cluster of outliers at a particular point in the dataset could also affect the median or mean. When some agencies are reporting data figures, they will filter out outliers, making their data more accurate.

Comparing apples with apples

When looking at median price, or any price data, it is important to remember that property sales represent a mix of house quality.

Renovated houses will sell for more than un-renovated property. Newer houses will sell for more than older ones (though in some areas older houses have charm and will sell for a higher price). Property in certain streets will sell for more than property in other streets. Properties with desirable features will get a better price. The area of land is also a factor and should be looked at as well.

If the market is selling homogeneously then these differences should not matter, as all sections in the market would be moving together. However, in some cases, one area of the market might fall independently of the rest of the market (e.g. during the GFC, the higher end of the market dropped in Sydney). Alternatively, buyers might have an increased preference for a particular section in the market (e.g. new houses with the introduction of a grant that applies to these exclusively).

Either of the above circumstances might skew data and affect the median price, making the overall market appear to move in one direction, but in reality, only one section of the market is affected. These factors should be considered when an investor is analysing price movements.

Over the long term, graphing the median price can reflect price trends, which is useful when examining the overall appreciation of the market over time.

Market trends

Educated investors will link the availability of money to house price trends across the entire market.

As discussed earlier, house prices follow the market fundamentals of supply and demand. The demand for houses will in turn follow the supply of money that is available to property buyers. When the supply of money increases (either through wage growth, higher employment, lower interest rates, government incentives, etc.) house prices will follow.

It has long been suggested (by the media, some demographers and others), that Australian house prices are 'over-inflated' and that Australia is in a 'housing bubble'. These commentators maintain that house prices are due for a downward correction. In fact, this has been repeated regularly throughout the GFC and is still probably being said.

With Australian house prices among the most stable in the world, and not suffering the same down-turn as in other economies, it would be easy to see how people may take this view, especially when house price rises are compared against increases in average Australian incomes. Overall, house prices have risen over the last 15 years disproportionately to incomes.

However, a different view may be seen when comparing house prices, not just to income alone but to affordability, as dictated by interest rates as well as income. The comparison shows a clearer trend, which, logically, perhaps better explains the relationship between price and the money supply fuelling housing's growth.

In Figure 8.2, the affordability of houses (determined by income alone, and determined by income plus interest rates) is graphed against median house prices. One point to note is the upward trend, and no indication of an unsustainable peak which might suggest an imminent crash.

Also worth keeping in mind is that this graph reflects the whole Australian property market, and it is inaccurate to think of the market as a whole.

Figure 8.2 – Median house prices (Australia) graphed against affordability index derived from average income and interest rates

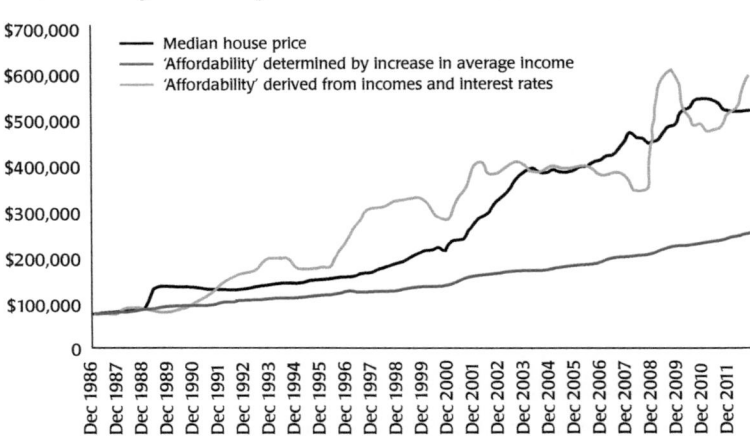

Data sources: REIA, ABS, RBA. © ResultsMentoring.com Reprinted with permission.

The housing market in fact consists of multiple sub-markets, which may move together but often move independently. There are several periods when the overall market has moved sideways (showing no real net growth) but it would have been wrong to assume that this meant that no *part* of the market was growing during this period. For an example of this, compare the period of 2003 to 2006 in Figure 8.2 above, and in Figure 8.1 for the Quirindi sub-market.

Affordability and money supply are two of many factors in a complex market dictated by a range of forces. Notwithstanding major economic upheaval, the future of the Australian property market would logically be set to continue for the next 15 years, as it has for the last.

Property market movements – fast and slow

One last factor to consider when examining house price growth is that, contrary to popular suggestion, prices do not increase uniformly over a set period of time.

Property prices tend to move upwards for a period, then remain stagnant (move sideways) for a period, before moving upwards again. As investors, we like to assume a standard growth in our calculations (e.g. 5% per annum for 10 years) but in reality, regular smooth growth does not occur.

Therefore to maximise our return from investments, we may need to factor in selling properties when we forecast that growth has slowed or will slow, and investing our cash into more productive properties in different markets.

Property growth reports and software

Property growth reports are an important tool in determining the right areas to invest. While past growth is not necessarily an indicator of future price movements, investors can use this information to help narrow down areas with potential for future gains. Equally, we can use growth data in combination with other information to help reaffirm our investing decisions. For information on resources available to investors for determining market growth, check out **www.achieveproperty.com/growth**.

CHAPTER SUMMARY

- House prices, like all prices, are dictated by the fundamentals of supply and demand.
- House price movements follow the supply of money that is used to buy the houses.
- The median house price is the 'middle' price in a set of house price data (e.g. within a suburb).
- As houses are bought with debt (mortgages) rather than cash, house price movements are more aligned to buyers' ability to access debt, than directly to wages (cash).
- Ability of home-buyers to access deposit money will also affect affordability. Schemes such as first home owner grants (FHOG) result in increased house prices as these improve affordability by increasing home-owner deposit funds access.
- The property market does not move up and down as one, rather there are multiple sub-markets that move independently.
- The property market often does not move uniformly, rather it may move quickly up over a period of months to years, then slowly over a period of years, before moving up again.

CHAPTER NOTES AND ACTIONS

Before moving on to the next chapter, spend a few minutes writing down the things that resonated with you from this chapter.

What actions do you need to take, or what do you need to plan to do, to help you get to the next level in your investing?

Write down at least 5 things now.

1. _____

_____

_____

2. _____

_____

_____

3. _____

_____

_____

4. _____

_____

_____

5. _____

_____

_____

9

VALUING A PROPERTY

- *A property is worth what someone will pay for it*
- *Property valuers give a value according to their valuation process*
- *There are many valuation options open to investors.*

In the previous chapter we saw how property prices move and we now have an understanding of some of the forces that drive growth in the property market. Does that mean that we can buy anything, and just wait for the money to come in? Unfortunately not.

Property investors make money when the value of the property rises, and the profit in the deal is the difference between the purchase price and the sale price (this is called the margin). It sounds simple but so many investors overlook the fundamentals of this process.

Some people say, "The profit is in the purchase", and to a degree this is true. If you overpay for a property at the start, then you have already prevented yourself from maximising your profit. Equally when you are selling a deal, you will always be under pressure to discount the price in order to move the property, so if you have bought well, it will make the selling process easier.

The last point here is important to remember: the seller has to sell but the buyer doesn't have to buy. The vendors want to sell their property but the buyers can buy anything. Therefore, it is always easier to get the vendor to negotiate on price.

So, what's a property worth?

How do we know what a property is worth? Properties aren't all the same and there is no listing for properties (as there is for shares on the sharemarket) telling us the price of a specific house at a specific time.

While the process of valuing can be quite complicated, establishing a property's true value is a very simple thing.

What a buyer will pay for it

The truth is that a property is worth what a buyer will pay for it. But, until a property actually sells, it is difficult to determine what the next person to buy it will actually pay for it. So we have property valuers whose job it is to make an educated guess at the price a house will sell for, if it sold in the current market.

What a property valuer values it at

You need to be aware that there are a couple of different types of valuer. In order for a lending institution to make a decision on how much to lend you, they will seek their own valuation of the property you are borrowing against. When a bank valuer is doing their job, they tend to be a bit conservative.

In most other circumstances, when a property is being valued at sale, the valuer will conclude that the value of the property is actually the market price (i.e. what the buyer is willing to pay).

Property valuers look at various statistics when establishing a property's value:

- They examine comparative sales of similar houses in the local vicinity
- They estimate the rental yield of the property, comparing average yields and then working backwards to a price

- They look at the last sale value of the property and market trends since
- They discount the price if the property needs repair or renovation
- They take into consideration the cost of renovations done since the last sale of the property
- They may perform an "in-line" discount (around 15%) if several properties are on a single title.

What an investor thinks the property is worth

But, how does the investor know what a property is worth? When an investor is buying a property, he or she has several options available to determine the value of a house.

1. **Getting an independent valuation done.** As we discussed in the previous section, an investor can pay a valuer to perform a valuation and give them an independent valuation of the property. This is a good way to accurately determine a likely value. But it costs money, and in most cases, investors don't go this far. For bigger projects, however, the costs of a professional valuation may well be worth it to offset the investor's risk.

2. **Seeking a real estate agent's appraisal.** This involves asking several real estate agents for an appraisal of the property's value (especially if you own the property and are looking to sell). It can be a good way of establishing an idea of the price. However, agents' valuations may be influenced by their desire to secure the listing, so keep this in mind – they may just be telling you what they think you want to hear. If several independent agents agree on the

approximate value of the property, then this can be a good indication of the potential market value.

3. **Knowing the current market.** One of the best ways to know the value of a property is to visit similar properties that are on the market, and when they sell, find out the sale price, and therefore have an idea of what your property is worth.

4. **Using valuation software.** The most useful tool for investors, when establishing property values, is online valuation software. In recent years, valuation software has come down in price dramatically. It used to be the domain of only real estate agents and savvy investors with real estate contacts. Now these software packages are readily available and there are many free or inexpensive options. Software that you pay for is still worth it, as these provide better accuracy and help the investor establish market trends. They also give historical price data for specific properties that helps in the negotiation process.

Of all the tools available to investors, good valuation software is probably the most cost-effective and useful. Readers seeking information and recommendations on valuation software should visit **www.achieveproperty.com/valuation**.

Valuation assists negotiation

With so many valuation options, then, what should a property investor do? The best recommendation is to use several of the above sources of information to establish the best true value that you can for the property you are buying. The more information you uncover the stronger will be your position when you start to negotiate with the vendor.

Personally, I use several valuation software packages and make use of local knowledge and agent appraisals. Where independent valuations are needed these will be done often during the initial due diligence period (before, or just after, an offer is made). This is generally for larger deals, not single houses.

With this knowledge, you are now equipped to be able to find the true values of properties you are looking at purchasing. Go to **www.achieveproperty.com/valuation** and check out the software options available.

CHAPTER SUMMARY

- The profit in the deal is the difference between the purchase price and the sale price.
- The seller has to sell their property but the buyer doesn't have to buy (they can buy anything). This means that often the seller has to move more on price than the buyer.
- A property's value is what it sells for to the next buyer.
- A valuer makes an educated "guess" as to what a property would sell for if it was sold in the current market.
- A property investor can determine a property's value using:
    1. An independent valuer
    2. A real estate agent appraisal
    3. Local market knowledge
    4. Valuation software
    5. Any/all of the above.

Links

For more information about valuation software, go to:
www.achieveproperty.com/valuation

Valuing a property

CHAPTER NOTES AND ACTIONS

Before moving on to the next chapter, spend a few minutes writing down the things that resonated with you from this chapter.

What actions do you need to take, or what do you need to plan to do, to help you get to the next level in your investing?

Write down at least 5 things now.

1. _____

   _____

   _____

2. _____

   _____

   _____

3. _____

   _____

   _____

4. _____

   _____

   _____

5. _____

   _____

   _____

10

LANDLORDING AND MANAGING TENANTS

- *There are five simple rules to follow when managing a property*
- *The golden rule is not to allow tenants to fall behind with their rent*
- *A good property manager can add value to your investment.*

The thought of being a landlord can be daunting. Sure, it is one thing to own your own home (that is scary enough) but having to be responsible for someone else's home is an even bigger responsibility. Worse still is the thought of having a tenant from hell who stops paying rent, trashes the property, then won't move out… that really is frightening!

Thankfully, most tenants are grateful to have a house to live in and treat their home with respect. They will pay rent on time and look after the property if you manage the process properly. There are also plenty of measures you can take to reduce the risk of damage or loss.

To make the process simple, we are going to cover the five rules of good landlording. Heed these rules and your life as a landlord will be manageable, but break the rules and be prepared for the consequences!

Rule #1 – Rent must be paid on time

The most common issue for landlords is a delay in being paid the rent they are owed, or not being paid at all! While most tenants are good – they pay regularly and on time – some tenants take advantage of landlord leniency and withhold rent.

Having a tenant in arrears has several implications for the landlord:

- It can affect your cash flow, which could be problematic for your investing business
- You will be charged interest on the loan repayments that the unpaid rent hasn't covered, (see the calculation at the end of this section)
- If a tenant defaults and vacates your premises, leaving rent in arrears, then the rent they owe may amount to the bond they have paid, meaning that any damage or repairs comes out of your own pocket.

The truth is that if a tenant gets into arrears, they are in effect borrowing from the investor, an interest-free non-securitised loan, for what may be an indefinite amount of time. In some cases this may quickly add up to hundreds or even thousands of dollars! If you are not prepared to loan your tenants $1,000 interest-free whenever they ask, then don't tolerate rental arrears!!

The best way to manage arrears is to prevent it happening. The problem lies in the tenant's false belief that rent money belongs to them. I prefer to see it as a situation where the rent has been 'purchased' and must be paid for, therefore the money for rent already belongs to the landlord, it is just awaiting changing hands.

Here's an analogy. If a person were to walk into a shop to buy milk and bread, but decided that they were going to pay for it in two weeks' time when they come in next (but they were still taking the bread and milk today), this would be called STEALING. But somehow we tolerate this behaviour when it comes to rental arrears.

The way to prevent a tenant from falling in arrears is to request that every tenant pays their rent as a direct deposit, which is set up when they first start renting. This makes sense for the tenant, as the money will automatically come out of their account, so they don't need to worry about going into a property manager's agency weekly to pay cash. They won't forget, it will happen automatically.

Most, if not all, banks will offer a free service where a tenant can set up a direct transfer from their account into the account of the property managing agency or the investor.

The only reason, thereafter, that a tenant will get into arrears is if they stop the direct debit, or if their account is empty of money. If the direct debit comes out of the account that they get paid into (or that their social security goes into) then they should never be without money to pay their rent. It is advisable that they set up their direct debit to happen shortly after, and at the same frequency as, when their income is paid.

Don't fall into the trap of reinforcing bad behaviour and allowing tenants to get into arrears. Investors who start out often want to be 'nice' to their tenants and be lenient when tenants get behind in rent for various reasons. The reality is that letting tenants get behind in their rent is teaching them bad financial skills and a lack of responsibility, which could get them into more trouble later in life. Be firm but fair. If a tenant gets behind, work with them and the property manager to coordinate a plan for them to keep paying their rent on time from now on, and to repay their arrears as quickly as possible. If they can't afford to pay, then they can't stay – and they need to be asked to leave.

When a tenant does get into arrears, it is usually because something has happened (they lose their job, break up with a partner, get sick, etc.) and the effort of coming in to pay rent, or find the money to pay rent, is greater than the incentive to do so.

Most tenants that get into arrears actually have the cash to pay their rent but choose not to, on the basis that they might want the money for something else. If the rent money has already been direct debited from a tenant's account, the temptation to withhold their rent money for other purposes isn't there.

This system will prevent a lot of stress and reduce the workload for both the investor and property manager.

> **READER QUIZ**
>
> Quick calculation question:
>
> If a tenant pays $350 per week rent, and is 2.5 weeks in arrears, for a 6 month period, what is the interest cost to the investor?
>
> For answers, see page 191

The answer may not seem like much, but if you have three tenants that are regularly behind in their rent, this is nearly $100 in interest you are paying. If you wouldn't pay $100 interest on your credit card, don't pay it on your tenant!

Rule #2 – Have adequate landlord's insurance

As a backup for when things do go wrong (and they will), a lifeline for investors is landlord's insurance. For investors who are starting out, full insurance is highly recommended. This includes building cover, contents cover and rental cover.

Rental cover will provide for tenant default (if they skip out and have rent owing), and loss of rent due to an issue that means the property is temporarily uninhabitable.

Building and contents cover should include damage that is accidental and damage or theft that is deliberate (e.g. caused by the tenant). There will be an excess to pay and this will be deducted from the amount of money that the insurance company pays you when you claim.

Having adequate insurance makes you feel better when something bad occurs because at least someone (the insurance company) is sharing the pain. If a tenant defaults and then skips town, your loss-of-rent cover will pay for the rental arrears and then the insurer will send a debt collector to try and recover the money from the tenant, so you don't have to.

As you become more experienced, you might decide to tweak your insurance to reduce your cover (and reduce your premiums) in some areas that you perceive as lower risk. But to start with, full cover is recommended.

Also highly recommended is the use of an insurance broker to help you find the best available insurance on the market for your situation. This will save you time and money. For more information on insurance brokers, check out **www.achieveproperty.com/insurance**.

Rule #3 – Use a property manager

Property managers are a cost of being a property investor. Yes, the cost at times seems high for what they do (anything from 4.5% to 8.8% of your rent paid) but the reality is that as an investor (especially if you are investing in your spare time) your time is better spent finding property deals and making money than trying to be cheap and saving money managing a property yourself.

Having said this, I recommend any investor starting out to consider managing their first couple of houses themselves for one to two years – if only to feel the pain of this task. That way, when they do outsource the job to an experienced property manager, they fully respect the person doing the job and understand what is involved. It also gives a good perspective on what needs to be done so they can bring their property manager into line if they are not doing the job properly.

A good property manager can add value to your investment in many ways, including:

- They will ensure that tenants pay rent on time (hopefully by setting up a direct debit as discussed earlier)
- They will regularly inspect the property and report on any repairs needed
- They will advise you of the market rent and when you are due for a rental increase, and provide photos as needed
- They will be able to recommend tradespeople for renovations and repairs, get quotes, and coordinate this process if necessary.

The property you are buying might be already tenanted and already managed by a local property manager. If this is the case, it might be easiest during the purchase period to keep the same manager when you buy the house.

If other investors who have properties in the area can recommend a particular manager that is probably the best help you will get in deciding which property manager to use. Otherwise, some questions you can ask when interviewing potential managers include:

1. How many properties do they have on their books?
2. How many property managers are there in the office?
3. Can your tenants be requested to pay by direct debit?
4. What is their policy when a tenant doesn't pay rent on time?

5. What is their protocol for going to the tribunal?
6. What is the cost?
7. What discount do they provide for an investor with multiple properties?
8. How often do they inspect the property for you?

As a rule, agencies with less properties on their books per manager are able to cope better. Tenants who get behind in rent should be followed up immediately with a telephone call and in writing as soon as possible. Tenants must understand that late payments are not tolerated.

The correct answer to (5) is "We have very few tenants who get taken to the tribunal as we do our job managing the property correctly." However, it is still good for the agency to have a procedure in place regarding how quickly tribunal applications are filed, etc.

Properties should be inspected at least every six months, and a full report provided.

Be good to your property managers as they have your asset in their hands.

Rule #4 – Be nice to your tenants

Perhaps the most important of the golden rules of good landlording is, "Be nice to your tenants". Contrary to popular belief, it is not the property that pays the landlord, but the tenant. Happy tenants will pay rent on time, will recommend other good tenants to a landlord, and will take care of a property. Unhappy tenants make for unhappy landlords.

Don't be tempted to withhold repairs on a property. If something needs fixing, have the repair done promptly. Depending on the repair, this may be a legal obligation of the landlord, but either way it will make for a satisfied tenant who is less likely to move out, and who will tolerate a rental increase better if they can see that their rent is going towards adequate maintenance.

Good tenants should be encouraged to stay, as much as bad tenants should be encouraged to go. Some exceptional landlords offer 'rewards' or 'incentives' to good tenants, such as vouchers or movie tickets at Christmas time. If you are doing a renovation, or in some way inconveniencing your tenant, consider a goodwill gesture at the end of the event. They will appreciate it and you never know how you might be repaid. As for when to tell your tenant about this 'incentive', and the reason for it, that is up to you. You might tell the tenant in advance that they will be getting the reward at the end of a renovation/construction, as an example (to help lessen the pain in the meantime). Or you might surprise them at the end, and they will be very appreciative.

Rule #5 – Manage the manager, manage your investment

The last golden rule of good landlording is to manage the manager. That is to say that while your property manager looks after your investment, you need to monitor them closely and ensure that everything is done appropriately. The most important part of the property manager–investor relationship, is communication.

Every month, your property manager will send you a statement of rent that has been paid, and the repairs (if any) that have been done. You must check this when it comes in and, if your tenant is in arrears or if there is anything you would question, contact the property manager immediately.

Keep track of your investment's financial figures on a monthly basis. In particular, you want to monitor the interest repayment, the rental income and any expenses. If you are losing money, then why is this, and what can you do to fix it? (We cover accounting and bookkeeping later in the book, so don't worry too much about this just for now.)

If there has been a delay in you being notified that your tenant is in arrears, ring the managing agent immediately and demand an explanation. A property manager should advise you as soon as a tenant gets two weeks in arrears with the rent. They should also send the tenant a letter immediately at this time. Let your manager know that it is imperative that they do their job properly. They are being paid (by you) not just to collect rent when it comes in and organise repairs, but to ensure that the investment runs smoothly, which means no arrears and a tenant who pays on time and looks after the property.

If your tenant gets behind with the rent, or vacates with arrears or with damage to the property, then you as the investor have to take responsibility. Don't blame the property manager, as it is your responsibility to manage the manager appropriately. However, if necessary of course, the property manager can be fired and replaced, if they really didn't do their job and if they can't learn from their mistakes. The best situation is where you can help your property manager to grow in their job, and improve their service to you and their other clients.

Most property managers are good at their jobs, and it is tough when tenants are in arrears. So be compassionate and try to see the situation from the property manager's point of view but also be firm and remember they are working for you.

Lastly, you should get a report from your property manager every six months about the property, after their inspection. The report should list everything and anything that needs repair. You should keep in contact with your property manager and determine if there is anything you can do to add value to the property for the tenant. This may enable you to raise the rent above the standard market increase. Examples of adding value include putting in air-conditioning, a new clothes line, landscaping improvements, etc.

You should personally visit the property every 12 to 18 months, even if you get consistent good reports from your property manager. Visits are tax-deductible.

CHAPTER SUMMARY

The five rules of good landlording – for successful landlording – are:

1. Rule #1 – Rent must be paid on time.
2. Rule #2 – Have adequate landlord's insurance
3. Rule #3 – Use a property manager
4. Rule #4 – Be nice to your tenants
5. Rule #5 – Manage the manager, manage your investment

Refer back to the chapter for more details if you need to and do not break these rules – ever.

Links

For further information about insurance brokers, visit: www.achieveproperty.com/insurance

CHAPTER NOTES AND ACTIONS

Before moving on to the next chapter, spend a few minutes writing down the things that resonated with you from this chapter.

What actions do you need to take, or what do you need to plan to do, to help you get to the next level in your investing?

Write down at least 5 things now.

1. _____
   _____
   _____

2. _____
   _____
   _____

3. _____
   _____
   _____

4. _____
   _____
   _____

5. _____
   _____
   _____

11

MAKING MONEY FROM PROPERTY INVESTING

- *Making money from investing will meet your initial reason for investing (refer back to Chapter 6)*
- *Property investing returns come in the form of cash flow or capital gains*
- *Value-adding is a sure-fire way to secure capital gains.*

Property investing is about making money. Many readers would have picked up this book because of its promise to help you learn how to make money in your spare time. Ultimately, being a property investor is about the creation of money for the purpose that your investing was started for – whether this was for financial freedom, to spend more time with family, for philanthropic purposes, to buy a house or whatever you desire!

There are three kinds of money that can be made from property investing. Depending on your reason for investing, you will want to focus on one or all of these. It will make more sense with some examples.

Three ways to make money from property investing

The three kinds of money from investing are:

1. Cash flow
2. Capital gains (realised)
3. Capital gains (unrealised)

Cash flow

You generate cash flow when a property investment produces a positive income stream, that is, the income (e.g. rent) from the property exceeds the expenses and after all expenses are paid the property makes money. In most cases, due to the high cost of mortgage interest, if a residential property is leveraged at 80% or higher it won't create much cash flow. Property that is owned outright (i.e. there is no mortgage) on the other hand could have significant cash flow potential.

Realised capital gains

Realised capital gains occur when a property increases in value and is sold. Any debts relating to the property are paid off and a profit remains. This profit may be subject to capital gains tax. The benefit of a realised capital gain is that the profit produced can be reinvested in future property deals or used for personal spending.

Unrealised capital gains

Unrealised capital gains occur when a property increases in value and is not sold, but instead is refinanced and the equity (the increase in value) is used to fund more investment purchases. Because the property has not been sold, this unrealised gain is not subject to tax (which is a benefit). However, because the equity has been created through financing, there will be interest to pay on this money (which is a cost). Unrealised capital gains should only be used for investment purposes (not personal spending) otherwise the interest component is not tax-deductible.

A money-making strategy

One of the secrets to starting investing and growing a property portfolio is to follow this sequence in your investing:

1. Buy a property at 80% or 90% LVR (and preferably buy at low-market value)
2. Add value to the property, e.g. by renovating
3. Refinance the property at its new value at 80% or 90% LVR
4. Extract your unrealised capital gain from the refinance and buy another property.

As long as the yield of the property is high enough to start with, you can refinance the property after value-adding and extract your initial cash, and it can still remain cash flow positive. Value-adding may also improve the rent return, helping the property remain cash flow positive after refinancing.

If your aim is to have a property portfolio generating cash flow, then you might find that you need to create capital gains initially and, once your portfolio is a suitable size, you may choose to pay down debt and use the cash flow from your debt-free or low-debt portfolio.

If your aim is to use property investing to create lump sums of cash (capital gains) then there are various techniques you can use for this. We will touch on these briefly later.

It is likely that in the course of your investing you will use all three kinds of money to grow your portfolio.

Whatever your property investing aim, you need to spend time planning your strategy, then set goals on what property you need to acquire (and what education you need first) in order to reach your goals.

Cash and property investing – what the banks don't tell you

As this chapter is about how to make money from property investing, it is worth touching on one of the greatest secrets in the property market – in fact, in the whole economy. This is 'fractional reserve lending'.

Understand this process and you will uncover the secret to growing a large portfolio and how to multiply your capital gains.

Money from property investing, as discussed, is made principally in two ways – either as cash flow or capital gains (the latter can be realised or unrealised). Both are important, but larger sums can be made from capital gains, provided the investor follows the right process.

When you buy a property, you take a loan (mortgage) for a set amount, with the goal that the property increases in value. At some point you sell the property, and pay off the loan, and any money that remains you keep (your profit is the difference between your mortgage and the new value at sale).

When your lender first gives you the loan, they will require that you contribute a percentage of the total value in cash (the deposit), and they will contribute the rest. For example, at an 80% LVR, the bank asks you to provide 20% (e.g. $40,000 on a $200,000 property) and they will provide 80% (the other $160,000).

Banks borrow and lend money all the time. When banks borrow money, this is often from people who have deposited their savings with the bank. The bank then pays an amount of interest in return for the deposited savings (often this is almost nothing when interest rates are low, like 0.1%, though it can be as high as 5% for some savings accounts). Banks then lend a proportion of this borrowed money to their customers as loans. A bank might lend 80% of deposited funds to borrowers, and the other 20% they keep as reserves, which is taken out of the monetary supply.

So a bank uses clients' savings, which they pay 0.1% interest on, and then charges their borrowers 7% interest for a mortgage, or 15%+ on outstanding credit card balances. You can see here how banks make their money.

Now, even though the bank has lent 80% of the depositors' funds to other people, the depositors still 'have' 100% of their money in the bank, and they are entitled to access it at any time. So long as not all the depositors want their money at once, the system holds up OK. The banks use their deposited reserve (e.g. the 20% in this case) to fund their day-to-day cash needs for withdrawals of deposits, paying interest, etc.

Using 'fractional reserve lending', banks collectively are actually able to lend *more* money than they borrow. The magic happens when the borrowed money is then *spent*, and the seller who receives the money deposits it in another bank and the process happens again. This way, the monetary supply can be expanded by sequential deposits and lending, and the system operates smoothly, provided a 'bank run' doesn't occur (where too many depositors want their money back at the same time).

The lesson to learn here is how banks use fractional reserve lending to make the most of their money, and how investors can use this to their advantage. Cash is the most important part of the transaction, which is why banks guard theirs so closely.

As an investor, your cash is one of your most limited resources, and if you want to grow your portfolio to its maximum (for greatest capital gains) you need to do what you can to release your cash so that you can use it for your next property deals.

The higher LVR you can get, the more property you can buy. If you can avoid unnecessary fees, taxes and costs, then you can have more cash for future purchases. Don't be afraid to spend money – this is an essential part of investing – but don't waste this resource either. And whenever you can, look for ways to get your cash out (through refinance or sale) to use it again to multiply your investment returns.

Ways to add value to a property

As we discussed earlier, a key component to making capital gains is value-adding. There are many ways to add value to a property, this is one of the advantages of investing in real estate. The secret is to add more in perceived value (what the buyer or tenant will pay) than in the actual cost, thereby you will make money.

Common ways to add value to property include renovating, landscaping, painting, de-cluttering and cleaning.

Less common ways to add value (which are potentially more profitable but also more advanced techniques) include developing, subdividing land, and strata-subdivision and property optioning.

We will briefly discuss the common ways of value-adding, as you will want to look for ways to value-add your first property investment. The less common ways will be covered in my next book! If you want more information on any of these techniques than is covered here, refer to Chapter Seventeen.

Renovating

Renovating is probably the most common form of value-adding for property investors. There are two forms of renovation:

- Cosmetic
- Structural.

Cosmetic renovations can involve significant work, but don't affect the integrity of the building. Structural renovations are a much bigger deal. They may need the involvement of structural engineers and may also require council approval. For beginner investors (and even the more experienced investors) cosmetic renovations are recommended for ease and efficiency.

When renovating, it is vital to have a firm idea of your end-sales value and work backwards. Establish what the property will be worth in its renovated form, or how much it will rent for once it has been renovated. The best way to determine this is to visit property that is on the market and has been renovated, and see what it then sells for. Alternatively, use valuation tools discussed in Chapter Nine.

> **HOT TIP FOR INVESTORS**
> In certain states, there are requirements for a seller to provide a building insurance certificate for renovation or building work over a certain value (e.g. $20,000). The builder should provide this and it is better to get the certificate at the time of completion of the work, instead of having to chase the builder several years later when you opt to sell. If you are doing a more major renovation, check with your solicitor if this is a requirement in your state.

Once you know your end sales price, get firm quotes on the cost of renovations and ensure that your profit margin will be there. It can be a bit of work getting quotes and I like to use a local handyman (or handyman/builder) to coordinate the trades and gather quotes, but you can do this work yourself, and for your first renovation(s) it is a good exercise to go through. It is important to get several quotes as you will be surprised at how prices can vary.

Areas that are most amenable to renovation include kitchens and bathrooms, but also living areas (depending on how they present).

Landscaping

Landscaping is a cost-effective form of adding value. But landscaping costs can blow out easily, so be sure to get a firm quote and understand how this work will lift the value of the property.

Where a garden is significantly overgrown, landscaping can change the entire character of the property. Adding a shed, or replacing a fence can also add value to a property.

There may be council restrictions on what can be done, and you may need to apply to council for a development approval (DA), depending on what you want to do. Generally, landscaping doesn't require approval, but chopping down trees might, and some fencing or sheds might also need council approval. Check council's website, or give them a call if you have questions.

Decorating

Painting and decorating is one of the most cost-effective ways to increase the value of the property. Neutral colours are a good idea for interior walls, and if necessary, speak to the painter or an interior designer for recommendations. Once you find colours that you like, feel free to use these for all your properties. I use standard variations of cream/beige/off-white for all my houses. Your local hardware store has sample sheets with colours on them, and there are now smart-phone apps for picking colours as well. Again, get several quotes as prices will vary among painters, but also it is worth getting recommendations from locals regarding who provides the best quality of work.

De-cluttering and cleaning

Some of the best opportunity properties on the market are houses for sale that are full of clutter and dirty. Home-owners don't like to buy houses that they cannot see themselves living in, so these properties present opportunities to investors who can buy at a discount.

If a house is full of junk (especially if it is a deceased estate sale) then be sure to specify in the contract whether you will dispose of the goods or if it must happen before settlement. If you will dispose of the goods, then you will want to specify if the goods are included in the sale or not. There can be considerable costs for removal of rubbish and disposal.

Remember to look UNDER the house. Often rubbish is stored here (if the house is on piers or stumps) and this can be a risk for pests, fire, etc., and all rubbish should be removed.

Subdividing land

OK, we said we wouldn't cover any of the less common ways to add value, however, you may come across a deal where subdivision has already been done, so it's worth a quick mention.

In my very first property deal that I told you about in Chapter One I bought a house that was on a large block which happened to be on two titles. This meant that the house was on one block of land but there was another block that didn't have a house on it, which was part of the sale. The second block had the driveway, landscaping, etc. and if you were looking at the house from the road, you would think it was just one big block of land, rather than two smaller blocks locked together.

As both blocks were on separate titles, this meant that someone who owned the property could build another house on the second block and sell it separately if they wanted to (and no subdivision work was needed as this had already been done). Or they could find a buyer who wanted a vacant block, and sell that, keeping the other. As a rule, two smaller blocks are worth more than one larger block, so there is potential for value here.

The more advanced technique is to find a large block on a single title and go through the process of adding value by actually seeking planning permission from the local council to divide the property into two smaller blocks and change to two titles.

Keep an eye out for this sort of situation when you are buying because, even if you don't subdivide, this may represent value to the next buyer who is interested in buying the house when you sell. (Look for either a house on two existing titles or one title where subdivision may be possible in the future.)

Last words on adding value

When adding value to a property, it is important to keep your target market at front of mind. Speak to local real estate agents about what is selling, and what buyers are willing to pay for at the time. It is easy to renovate or develop a property but then fail to get your price if you do not create something that is in demand.

Finally, you will only add value if you don't pay too much to start with. A property that needs value-adding (e.g. renovating, landscaping, painting or other repair) will be harder to sell, so you may have an opportunity to negotiate harder. Be sure to mention to the selling agent just how much you feel it will cost to fix it up (i.e. a lot of money!), and this is a reason that (understandably) you cannot pay top dollar for the property.

Calculating an expected profit from a property investment

The most important part of planning a property purchase is doing the sums to be sure that your deal is profitable. When looking to create a capital gain, consider the price that the property will sell for, after value has been added. If you are renovating the property, look at comparative prices for properties that have been similarly renovated and (crucially) have sold. Recent sales in the area that you are looking at will give a reasonable indication of the price you might expect to sell for.

From the estimated end-sale price, then work backwards.

Add up:

1. The price you expect to pay to buy the property
2. Any purchase (closing) costs
3. The costs of renovating the property
4. Any holding costs (for example, the cost of the mortgage interest)
5. Agent commissions for sale (if you intend to sell).

Subtract the five costs above from the estimated end-sale price and you have your likely profit before tax (provided there are no further unforeseen costs).

READER QUIZ

Calculate the profit you would make if you can carry out this project.

The end-sale price has been estimated at $320,000 (assume no rent comes in during the six month period).

(a) The price for buying the property $250,000
(b) Any purchase (closing) costs 5% =   _____
(c) The costs of renovating the property
    10% of purchase price =   _____
(d) Any holding costs (for example the
    cost of the mortgage interest) 7% interest
    at an 80% LVR for six months =   _____
(e) Agent commissions for sale (if you intend
    to sell) 4% of end-sale price =   _____

What did you think after running these numbers? How does the deal look on paper? Would you do this deal? What could you do to make this project more profitable?

For answers see page 191

Take into account rent if there will be rent paid during this period as this can add to your profit. You can factor in expected market appreciation or depreciation, too, but be realistic rather than overly optimistic. At the end of this exercise you have an indication of whether your investment project will be profitable or not.

The secret to making money from property investing is to know your costs and values, and ensure that projects run to plan. Especially when doing your first couple of deals, it is easy to pay too much, and to over-capitalise (spend too much) on renovations. It is also easy to underestimate the time it can take for things to happen. All of these issues can result in cost blow-outs and lost profits. But if this does happen, don't get overwhelmed! This happens to everyone! This is the reason why it is recommended to take on a couple of small projects initially to limit learning mistakes to smaller amounts of money and time. Once you have gained some experience, move up to bigger projects.

Depreciation allowances

One last point to mention when you are looking at renovations and other similar add-value projects, (as well as all your properties – even the unrenovated ones) is the usefulness of getting a quantity surveyor's report done for depreciation purposes. Quantity surveyors will physically inspect your investment and let you know the value of everything in your property. This inspection will then allow you to claim depreciation on all the items of the property where this is possible.

Getting a quantity surveyor's report before a major renovation can allow the investor to write off items that are replaced. After the renovation, new items can also be depreciated over time. The person to speak to initially about this process, and how it can help your investing, is your accountant.

Depreciation is 'tax-deferral' because the money you save and offset against the tax you pay will eventually be added to your cost base when you sell and then you pay capital gains tax on any profit (if appropriate). The benefit is that in the short-term you can use this to optimise your cash flow and with the tax saved you can reinvest this cash in other investments.

Visit **www.achieveproperty.com/quantitysurveyors** for further information on quantity surveyors.

CHAPTER SUMMARY

- The three kinds of money from investing are:
    1. Cash flow
    2. Capital gains (realised)
    3. Capital gains (unrealised)
- When you are buying property, you should buy with a focus on securing equity from the start, and then adding further capital through improvements or value-adding.
- Fractional reserve lending is the principle where banks lend more money than they have, and this expands the economy through leverage. Investors should take this principle of leverage into account when planning their investing strategies – the same techniques can be used to expand an investor's portfolio.
- There are many ways to add value to a property, including:
    - Renovations
    - Landscaping
    - Painting
    - De-cluttering and cleaning
    - Developing
    - Subdividing land
    - Strata-subdivision

If you are looking for more specific information on the strategies listed here, see Chapter Seventeen.

Links

For more information on Quantity Surveyors, visit:
www.achieveproperty.com/quantitysurveyors

CHAPTER NOTES AND ACTIONS

Before moving on to the next chapter, spend a few minutes writing down the things that resonated with you from this chapter.

What actions do you need to take, or what do you need to plan to do, to help you get to the next level in your investing?

Write down at least 5 things now.

1. _____

   _____

   _____

2. _____

   _____

   _____

3. _____

   _____

   _____

4. _____

   _____

   _____

5. _____

   _____

   _____

12

SEARCHING FOR AND FINDING THE RIGHT PROPERTY

- *The first step is to narrow down your search criteria*
- *Price isn't the only thing when searching for property*
- *Finding low value property will kick-start your capital gains.*

In 2006, at the last census, there were 7.8 million households in Australia, with hundreds of thousands of properties for sale nationwide on any given day. With this many properties to choose from, how does an investor know what to purchase?

There are several factors to consider when narrowing down your search on what to buy. We are going to work through a few decisions you need to make, and for the purpose of this chapter, let's assume that the investor is wanting to make a capital gain from the investment (either realised or unrealised).

When selecting the kind of property to focus your search on, it is important to do so with your investing goals in mind. What do you want to achieve? This will help you focus on the kind of property that will get you closer to your goal.

Narrow down the selection criteria

We start by narrowing down a few selection criteria. In the space below, write your answers to the questions (don't worry you can revise this later).

1. What is your price range? (I recommend under $200,000 for a first property purchase, even under $100,000 is suggested)

   _____

2. In which state or area do you want to buy? (I suggest the state you live in, for an initial purchase)

   _____

3. What's your preferred location — CBD, city suburb or large regional centre?

   _____

4. House or unit? (This might depend on your personal preference, also what is available in your price range in the location you are currently opting for)

   _____

5. Rental yield — what percentage of the purchase price should the rent bring in, per annum?

   _____

6. What do you want to do with the property (e.g. Buy → add-value → hold, or Buy → add-value → sell)? Don't worry about how you will add value, unless you already have an idea, just choose whether you think you want to hold the property for a year or more, or sell it quickly and move on.

   _____

7. Who do you have in mind when you are buying the property (e.g. who will you rent it to, or sell it to — what is your target market)?

   _____

Having answered these questions, you will at least have some idea of what you are after, where you are going to find it, and how much it is going to cost. Then you have a reasonable idea of what to do when you buy it. Excellent work.

If you can find a property in an area you are happy with, for the right price, then you are on your way to getting your first investment.

Before you start looking, we will touch on a few key considerations when looking for where to find suitable investment properties.

Buying a property at the right price

> This is possibly the most important section of this book – so don't skip over it!

The goal for every investor when buying a property should be to create a win-win situation with the vendor, where both parties get what they want. As an investor we should never be aiming for a scenario where one party wins and the other loses.

At the end of the transaction, when we have bought a house, we have done the vendor a service by buying a property from them that they needed to sell. Equally, they have done us a service by selling a property that we want to buy. Having purchased the property, our goal as the investor is then to add value to it in some way to make a profit from the transaction.

Many investors fail to realise this is how it works (win – win). As a result, they pass up great opportunities because seeing the potential for profit, they feel that they are *winning* and the seller is *losing*, so they don't pursue the deal any further.

Alternatively, an investor might see the advertised price for a property and, recognising that it is too high for them, they might pass up the deal and instead look for another one. In both of these situations, because the investor hasn't approached the vendor to at least *ask* some more questions from them, they are actually disadvantaging the vendor.

It might be hard to believe but price isn't necessarily the most important thing to all sellers. One element of creating a good capital gains deal can be locating a property that is selling at low market value. Properties sell every day at prices that are lower than the average property sells for and this is because the seller places more importance on factors other than price. For a seller to 'win' it doesn't necessarily mean getting the highest price.

This can be a difficult concept to appreciate for investors who are starting out. When you eventually find yourself in a situation where you need to sell a property, and price isn't the most important thing to you, then you will understand.

The joy of a reduced price

Do you remember a situation when you have discovered the joy of shopping in a department store or supermarket and have found a particular item you have been looking for and it is on special or has a price reduced sticker? Maybe it was an older model, or the packaging was a bit faded, but it was just what you wanted and you got it at a great price because the shop-keeper just wanted to clear the stock.

This works for property as well. The longer a property stays on the market, the harder it is to get top price for it, because it becomes devalued in the eyes of the market. If a house isn't selling, then people generally might start to think there is something wrong with it, or no-one wants it, so it's got to be worth less. The longer a property sits on the market, the more likely a vendor might be flexible on price, especially if they really need the cash for something else or they need to sell for a particular reason.

By assuming that the advertised price on a property is as low as the vendor will accept, you may actually be doing the seller a disservice by not negotiating with them, and just passing up the deal. Their property may remain unsold for months, or even years, because no one has approached them to buy it at a lower price than what it is advertised for.

One of the biggest things for a new investor to learn is that just because the buyer (you) is price-focused doesn't mean that everyone else is too. Vendors (sellers) will often sell at a lower price because of reasons such as:

1. They just want to sell quickly.
2. They have serious time constraints and need a guaranteed sale by a particular date.
3. They want to sell for emotional reasons and money is less important than just getting the house sold.
4. They are not emotionally attached (or unattached) to the property.
5. It is a mortgagee sale (where the bank has foreclosed and needs to shift the property off its books).
6. It is a deceased estate and the estate wants a fast sale.
7. There is no mortgage owing, so nothing to pay off, and some flexibility on price.
8. There has been little to no interest in the property and the vendor is willing to drop the price so it will sell.
9. The vendor doesn't want people coming through the property and will sell at a lower price to avoid an open listing.

The most important thing when talking to the agent selling the property is to ascertain the reason that the vendor is selling. This will give insight into why the property is on the market and how flexible the seller is on price.

If you can discover the vendor's reason for selling (their real reason) and you can offer them terms to satisfy this need, then they may well be happy to reduce the price to sell the property to you.

At all times, it is the vendor's choice whether they accept your offer or not, so don't feel that you can't offer a lower price because you think they won't accept. The worst they can do is say no, which is fine – they can sell their property to someone else, if there is someone else who can satisfy their needs and meet their price.

Having said this, the technique isn't to go around making hundreds of low-ball offers in the hope that one will be accepted. Instead, identify properties where the vendor may be interested in accepting a lower market value offer, in order to help move the property off the market quickly, and ask lots of questions to identify the opportunity and the vendor's real needs. Then make an offer at a fair, but low-market, price while simultaneously offering terms that suit the vendor, in order to gain acceptance.

A fair but lower offer might be 15% to 20% below what the property might otherwise sell for, over a three to four month period, if it were presented in the best possible way (e.g. renovated, cleaned and well-marketed). Also ensure you deduct from your offer the cost of the improvements needed – for example the costs of renovation and cleaning if this is required.

Search strategies for low-market-value properties

Properties that will sell at the lower end of market value may not be easy to find. Keep in mind that when we say 'low market value' we don't mean the low end of the entire market, we are talking about low-market-*value* properties, that is properties that sell at a price that is at the lower range for *their* market. These kind of properties will exist in all areas of the property market. The amount of discounting that occurs will depend on the motivation of the seller to sell.

Given that these properties may be hard to find, where do we look to find them? They can be found anywhere that standard properties are found – online at **www.realestate.com.au**, or **www.domain.com.au**, in the classifieds section of newspapers (print and online), in real estate agent's windows, and they can also be found by word of mouth, etc.

On the surface, these properties may also appear just like any other property. To identify them, we need to look at the vendor's reason for selling. You might find some hints that the property will sell at low market value if it is listed with keywords like "vendor must sell", "mortgagee sale", "bank says sell", "forced sale", "all offers considered," etc.

Equally, properties that are not well-presented may be struggling to attract offers. These properties also reflect a vendor that may not be motivated on price, because they have not done what is necessary to bring the property to a more marketable standard. Examples of properties that are not well presented are those with lots of clutter, in need of paint, where the yard is in severe need of gardening, etc.

Properties that have remained on the market for a long period of time are also potentially going to sell at a lower market value. They may have remained on the market for various reasons, some may have been listed above. Sometimes the vendor just has an unrealistic expectation on price and you probably aren't interested in these deals either.

One way to identify these properties is to contact all the real estate agents in your area and tell them specifically what you are after. Ask them if they have anything that fits your criteria. Obviously, in order to do this, you will need to have worked out your area and decided on the price range and other criteria you are looking for.

If you tell an agent that you are a property investor and you are ready to buy (one or more houses) right now, then agents will usually be helpful in finding prospective deals for you. Some agents will require a little convincing but after you have purchased a couple of houses they are usually very motivated to bring more properties to your attention.

A great question to ask agents is, "Do you have any properties that are not selling?" or, "I am interested in mortgagee sales," or, "I am interested in properties that are likely to sell at low (or below) market value". Not all agents will get mortgagee sales so don't be surprised if some say that they simply don't carry these sorts of properties.

Forming relationships with local agents

This is one of the best ways to get good property deals before other people even hear about them. In some cases you might be told by an agent about properties for sale before they are even advertised.

Using software and search engines

Another very effective means of locating properties at low market value is by using software or search engines designed for property investors. These software systems are becoming more common but are still very under-utilised. Generally you will pay a fee for a subscription and then be able to use the software online. The fee may be a few hundred dollars for a few months, or a thousand dollars+, for a year or more. The potential benefit is being able to locate property that is discounted which may mean you can make tens of thousands or even hundreds of thousands of dollars in instant equity when you purchase. Not only is this a good way of making money but it also can be a good way of quickly growing a property portfolio.

A successful investor knows how to find the right property and the right vendor, and ask the right questions, so that they can make the right offer that satisfies the vendor's needs. By meeting their needs, we may then find the vendor is flexible on price. Creating a win-win outcome is always our number one objective.

Visit **www.achieveproperty.com/searchtools** for information on tools you can use to find discounted or low-market-value property.

CHAPTER SUMMARY

- Finding the right property is about narrowing down your search to specifically what you are after. Use the questions in this chapter to help in this process.

- Price isn't the most important thing to all sellers. (Many investors struggle with this point.) If you can solve a seller's problems then they may be more than happy to sell to you at a better price.

- Low market value properties can be found using a variety of strategies. Try some of these and you might be surprised at how many "good deals" are available in the current market.

Links

Some property search software I have researched can be found at: www.achieveproperty.com/searchtools

Searching for and finding the right property

CHAPTER NOTES AND ACTIONS

Before moving on to the next chapter, spend a few minutes writing down the things that resonated with you from this chapter.

What actions do you need to take, or what do you need to plan to do, to help you get to the next level in your investing?

Write down at least 5 things now.

1. _____

    _____

    _____

2. _____

    _____

    _____

3. _____

    _____

    _____

4. _____

    _____

    _____

5. _____

    _____

    _____

13

THE IMPORTANCE OF THOROUGH DUE DILIGENCE

- *It is your responsibility, if you purchase property, to conduct thorough due diligence*
- *There are experts who can help you with this to uncover any potential problems with a property*
- *Don't skip ANY of the due diligence process.*

One of the most profound laws of property investing is the Latin warning "caveat emptor" which means "buyer beware". After a property has been sold, unless the seller has actively concealed a fault, the buyer generally has no recourse against the seller for imperfections or issues down the track.

For first-time investors this can be a scary thing. What if the property you are buying has something wrong with it that you don't detect, due to a lack of experience? Add to this the fact that the property that investors buy is often older, or in need of renovation. You need to be able to distinguish between things that are minor issues and things that are major and will be expensive to repair (or get worse).

The good news is that major problems uncommonly occur, so long as you undertake a process of thorough due diligence and there are plenty of experts who can help you with this process for a very reasonable cost.

Note that there will be problems that happen when you are investing in property. They cannot be avoided and are part of property investing. But there are strategies that you can put in place to keep them to just 'annoying' rather than 'disastrous'.

What is due diligence?

Due diligence is a legal/accounting term relating to the investigation of a business or property or person, prior to entering into a contract (e.g. prior to a company acquisition, or a partnership, merger, etc.). The term is also used in real estate and property investing, prior to the purchase of a property.

During the due diligence period we undertake all the investigations necessary to ensure that property is how we think it is, and that there are no issues that have gone undetected. This period generally occurs after an offer is accepted, but before a contract is exchanged (or before a contract goes unconditional, depending on the state where you are purchasing). This means that you will generally have a 'back-out' clause, so that you can exit the deal with little cost if you find something seriously wrong with the property.

During this process, if you happen to uncover something that you didn't know about when you made your offer – don't worry! If it is a deal-breaker, advise the agent that you won't proceed and let them know why, and get your goodwill deposit back.

If it's a minor issue but is still costly to put right, approach the agent and advise them that this needs to be fixed by the vendor prior to exchange of contracts, or have the price changed so that you can fix the item yourself after settlement. If you are going to renegotiate on price, it is worth doing this through your solicitor but let the agent know what is happening and why. Your solicitor will talk to the vendor's solicitor, who will talk to the vendor, and then the whole communication will happen in reverse.

Before you go to the other side with this suggestion for change in purchase price, ensure you get several quotes, but use this to your advantage (within reason) as a negotiating tool. It is also possible to have written into the contract that the vendor will fix the issue after contract exchange and before settlement. There are lots of options and the idea is to continue to create a win-win for both sides. It is possible that the vendor will refuse, so have a plan as to what to do if this happens.

Don't worry about your lack of experience in the area of due diligence when you are buying your first property. Every investor who is starting out lacks experience – this is one reason why I suggest your first couple of property investments are of a lower price, so that any mistakes you do make are limited. You can always employ professionals to do inspections for you that will uncover any issues. This is a way of safeguarding against hidden problems.

Due diligence inspections

There are various types of inspections required when considering buying a property. Some of these inspections cost money and this is an expected cost of property investing. Do not skip any of these steps – ever. Following this simple rule will help ensure that you don't risk a significant loss by making a critical mistake or missing something important.

When it comes to deciding who to use for building and pest inspections there are several people who can give recommendations. The agent selling the property is usually very helpful in providing names of local professionals. Ask for a few recommendations for a builder and pest inspector. You can also ring up other property managers or agents and ask them for recommendations too. If you know of other investors who have bought in the area, they may also suggest who to use.

Building inspections

Every property should have an independent building inspection done before contracts become unconditional. *You* should do an initial inspection first, and if the property looks reasonable to you, then follow up with an inspection by a licensed building inspector.

Pest inspections

Every property should also have a pest inspection done. There are a variety of pests that can affect houses and your pest inspector will advise on the risks and what can be done (if anything is necessary) to minimise the risks to your investment.

Local area inspections

This is something that you will want to do, familiarise yourself with the area, your immediate neighbours and the streets around the property you are buying. You don't need to buy the worst house in the best street but you don't want to buy the best house in the worst street. In fact, you don't want to buy any house in the worst street. Talk to a few property managers from local real estate agents and find out what areas to avoid (they will know). A good litmus test is whether a property manager will take on the property. If an area is bad enough that they won't manage the house, this might be a reason not to buy it.

Inspecting the profitability of the deal

Outlined in Chapter Eleven is the process of determining the profit or equity in a property you are considering buying following a renovation or other value-add. Checking the numbers is a vital part of your due diligence process because you must be sure that the investment will be profitable from day one. Ensure that the house you are looking at buying has both value-add potential (or that you are buying at a low market value, or both) and that the area has growth potential as well. Speak to several property managers in the area and ensure that the rent you expect is achievable, and that the property will be easy enough for them to tenant and manage.

Inspect the contract for sale

You should use a solicitor to review the contract before you sign. Never sign a contract in front of a real estate agent, or in their office (despite their protestations that you should). Your solicitor needs to review all contracts before you sign. You should also read the contract thoroughly yourself and get used to what contracts say – this is part of your education. Sit down with your solicitor and get them to explain what the different sections in the contract mean.

The contract will advise of issues relating to the block of land that your property is situated on. There may be building restrictions that will affect future development, there may be flood risks or other issues that you need to be aware of. Ask your solicitor to point out if there are any problems that you need to know about.

Plumbing, electrical and other inspections

Depending on the age and state of repair that your property is in, you might want to engage other inspectors for specific areas that may need consideration.

If the property is new and if your building inspection doesn't turn up any issues then it is quite likely that plumbing, electrics and gas are all OK. If the house is old and in need of renovation, or if it has been damaged by a previous occupant, then you might want electrical and plumbing inspections as well.

If the water and plumbing are turned off then you may find some issues that cannot be detected during inspection. Consider accounting for this in the price you offer. You can still ask for an inspection during this time, and you may still receive some useful advice.

It's not unusual for a builder, plumber or electrician in a smaller town, to already have knowledge of the property you are purchasing (as they may have been called there before). They may even be able to give you some idea of the property's state of repair, even without seeing it again.

Plumbers will often give a property a once-over and verbally advise if anything needs further attention. Electricians also may not charge for a quick inspection. There are several things you can look at yourself:

- If the meter box looks new and has new switches, then it is likely that the property has been re-wired, and this is good. If the meter looks really old, and so too do the light switches and power-points, maybe ask an electrician for advice on whether re-wiring could be something needed in the future (as this is costly).
- Turn on the water taps as you inspect the kitchen, bathroom, laundry, etc. and listen for water-hammer (this is a boom-boom-boom sound as you quickly turn on or off a tap). This may be an indication that pipes need inspecting.

- Look out for water stains around and under sinks, in the roof, etc., that might indicate leaks.
- Check the age of the hot water system, and if it is getting on, then it may need replacing during your ownership.

There are many more things you can learn about property inspections and the best place to learn these things is by reading books, attending courses and seminars, and getting out and inspecting properties. You will see more information on this when you get to Chapter Eighteen.

You don't need to be an expert when you buy your first investment property, so don't let inexperience hold you back. Do a thorough inspection yourself first. Arrange a pest and building inspection next, and ask your inspectors lots of questions and follow up anything you need to. Have your solicitor review the contract and make any changes necessary. Be happy with the numbers in the deal and be happy with the area.

If you feel you still need more help, that's fine, get some more property education or find a property investing mentor (see Chapter Eighteen). The important thing is to get started.

CHAPTER SUMMARY

- Due diligence is the name given to a vitally important part of the property buying process where the buyer thoroughly investigates all aspects of the purchase to ensure that they are buying exactly what they think they are buying (and that there are no concealed problems or overlooked issues).
- Various inspections need to be done during this period, including, but not limited to:
    - A building inspection
    - A pest inspection
    - A local area inspection
    - Inspecting the profitability of the deal
    - Inspecting the contract
    - Plumbing, electrical and other inspections.
- Use your team of knowledgeable tradespeople and professionals to carry out and advise you on these inspections.

CHAPTER NOTES AND ACTIONS

Before moving on to the next chapter, spend a few minutes writing down the things that resonated with you from this chapter.

What actions do you need to take, or what do you need to plan to do, to help you get to the next level in your investing?

Write down at least 5 things now.

1. _____
   _____
   _____

2. _____
   _____
   _____

3. _____
   _____
   _____

4. _____
   _____
   _____

5. _____
   _____
   _____

14

SERVICING YOUR LOAN

- *As your portfolio grows, serviceability can become more of a challenge*
- *You can improve your income from paid work*
- *You can also improve your income through investing in cash flow property.*

Serviceability is your ability to make the repayments on the loan you have agreed to take (to buy your property). We talked about serviceability in Chapter Five (Securing Enough Finance) and we come back to it here because it stands out as a concern for property investors.

Serviceability may be less of an issue for property investors who are just starting out and are buying their very first property, but servicing your loans is still something worth working through, especially if you are planning to increase your portfolio fairly quickly. As the size of your portfolio grows, you will see that this needs to be done right to allow continued expansion.

When we talked a little bit about serviceability earlier in the book, we didn't go into how you can use it to your advantage to build your portfolio in such a way as to maximise your ability to borrow.

Increasing your income

For investors on lower salaries, or who are self-employed, it may be harder to service a loan, as the banks may be wary of your limited income. Therefore, in order to overcome this, you will need to either get a new job (with a higher salary, or with an employer rather than be self-employed, etc.) or find another way to have income coming in to fund your mortgage interest. Some possibilities for this include:

1. Finding a joint venture partner with a higher salary and doing the deal together (using their serviceability instead of, or as well as, yours)
2. Finding a property with a high enough rent that will cover the mortgage and all costs (i.e. a positive cash flow property)
3. Using other income, for example from another business or other property to offset the interest on the property you are buying.

There are likely to be many more creative ways to help improve your serviceability and the more you can use lateral thinking, the more you can potentially expand your ability to grow your property portfolio. Several friends of mine are great at using creative finance and partnerships to fund their property business and their financial freedom.

Income from your property

What is worth keeping in mind is that a major factor in serviceability is the income produced by the property itself. Negative gearing is a strategy that has been popular over the last 20 years due to perceived tax benefits. However, the biggest risk from this strategy is that you need to make a loss on the property in order to receive the tax deduction. If you are making a loss, you are *paying* money, therefore what do you think this does for your ability to service more loans?

On the other hand, buying property that is cash flow positive means that instead of paying money you have income coming in.

One of the fundamentals to building a larger portfolio is to source property that has a higher yield, preferably with positive cash flow. Therefore, the income generated by the property will help offset the interest requirement for your next purchase. If you keep buying positive cash flow property, then in theory, you can keep building a portfolio indefinitely!

Interest-only loans versus principal and interest loans

It is important to remember that to 'service' a loan, you need to be able to demonstrate to the bank that you can *repay the amount of money* that you have agreed to. Now, there are two kinds of loans and we haven't really discussed these yet. A loan can be either Interest Only (IO) or Principal and Interest (P&I). They mean pretty much what they say. IO loans are where you only repay the interest while with a P&I loan you pay interest and also pay down some of the amount you borrowed each month. The benefit of a P&I loan is that the interest eventually starts to drop so your investment becomes more cash flow positive. However, the disadvantage is that this kind of loan is more draining on your cash flow in the short-term.

In the 'good old days' all loans used to be P&I and no one thought any different. People used to invest in property for the long term and would pay down their loan over ten or twenty years. That was just how it was done.

In the world today, things are very different. Property investors very rarely use P&I loans. Instead, loans are taken out often as interest-only for five years then refinanced at the end of this period for another period of interest-only. The principal isn't paid off (so you are paying a higher amount of interest over the life of the loan, which unsurprisingly the banks are quite happy with).

The benefit to the investor for this kind of finance is twofold. Firstly, it is easier to service this kind of loan because you need less cash coming in (in the short term) to just pay the interest rather than having to pay down the principal as well. The second advantage is that the investor can then redirect the money they would otherwise have had to use for principal repayments and use this for an additional property purchase instead. You might be able to buy two properties with IO loans where you could only have afforded one with a P&I loan.

While saving for the next property, it is a good idea to use an offset account so that any money that is currently not being used for deposits or working capital can be used to reduce the interest that you pay on one or more of your loans. This is not the same as adding money to the loan and then drawing down on it. Talk to your broker about setting up an offset account for the loan on the next property you purchase. Make sure that your offset account is 100% offset – but these days most are.

The key message for this chapter is that when you are considering your first property, or first several property deals, if you are looking at buy-and-hold as a strategy (to keep the property for at least a year or more) then take into account the yield that you are looking for, and think about how this might affect your ability to service further purchases in the near future. By using means to maximise your serviceability you will be able to grow your portfolio faster.

Think about how big a portfolio of properties you want to build and what strategies or techniques you will need in order to keep growing and servicing your portfolio. It is worth spending some time on this, especially if you want a large property portfolio.

Don't worry if nothing comes to mind just yet. (But if it does – write it down!) Keep reading on and we will look at this in some more detail in later chapters as well.

CHAPTER SUMMARY

- Serviceability is your ability to repay the interest on the loan that you agreed to.
- If you cannot service a loan, alternatives include:
  - Find a joint venture partner with a higher salary.
  - Find and invest in cash flow positive property.
  - Use income from other businesses or more positive cash flow property to offset the interest in the property you are buying.
- Consider an interest-only loan for better serviceability and use an offset account to reduce the interest you pay, if you have spare money between investment property purchases.
- When starting out, one of the keys to getting a portfolio off the ground is solving the serviceability issue.

CHAPTER NOTES AND ACTIONS

Before moving on to the next chapter, spend a few minutes writing down the things that resonated with you from this chapter.

What actions do you need to take, or what do you need to plan to do, to help you get to the next level in your investing?

Write down at least 5 things now.

1. _____
   _____
   _____

2. _____
   _____
   _____

3. _____
   _____
   _____

4. _____
   _____
   _____

5. _____
   _____
   _____

15

STRUCTURING HOW YOU PURCHASE INVESTMENT PROPERTY

- *Structuring can influence the tax you pay and how well your assets are protected*
- *Different structures are more costly to set-up and run*
- *You should take financial and legal advice before you make structuring decisions.*

Structuring has nothing to do with the physical property. Walls, floors and roofs are all structural parts of the property but this is not what we are talking about when we discuss structuring in this context.

In these last couple of chapters, we are going to touch on some legal and accounting information, so it is timely to remind you again that this is general information and does not constitute specific advice. You should seek professional legal or accounting advice when considering the best way of organising your portfolio. As laws are constantly changing, it is possible that some of the details discussed here could become out-of-date, and there can be variations between states and countries. If you are looking at setting up a specialised structure (e.g. a company, trust or some such variation) then you will need to talk to your accountant and solicitor, and you may wish to speak to your finance broker as well.

For recommendations on legal and accounting advisers, go to **www.achieveproperty.com/advisors**.

What is structuring?

So, why am I dedicating a chapter to this thing called structuring? The term 'structuring' refers to the entity that you purchase your property with.

An entity may be you, as an individual, and so you will buy property in your personal name. It could be a company, a trust, or other variations on these. There are many different entities that you can use to buy property, and depending on how you go about purchasing, there may be different tax implications and different levels of asset protection, as well, offered as a consequence.

Often you will use more than one entity to create the best structure. The design of your structure may also have an effect over how easily you can get finance, and the cost for set-up and ongoing fees. If it sounds like there is a lot to cover, there is. But this is why you have good advisers! This chapter aims to offer an overview of your options so that you can seek professional advice coming from a more knowledgeable position.

Tax implications

When I talk about tax implications, this means that depending on what entity or structure you use to buy your property, you might be taxed differently while you hold the property and when you sell.

Asset protection

Asset protection means choosing an entity or structure to buy your properties in, so that in the (hopefully unlikely) event that someone decides to sue you, your assets (properties) remain safe. Good asset protection means that if you were sued personally your properties would not be easy for someone to try and lay claim over. When you have one house this is important, but it is perhaps even more of a priority when you own several million dollars worth of real estate.

Let's look at a few different structures or entities and some of the benefits and costs of each.

Ownership in your own name

The simplest way to buy property is in your own name. Anyone can use their own name to buy property, there are no set-up costs, no ongoing costs and relatively few issues. When it comes to doing your annual tax return, there will be a bit more to add, but that's OK. Another benefit of buying in your own name is that if you do happen to make a loss from your property, you can offset this against your taxable income (you will need to talk to your accountant about this). Borrowing may also be easier as banks are very comfortable with this structure.

Millions of people across Australia use this structure when buying property. There are also capital gains discount advantages that can be a benefit when property is held in your own name for a period of longer than 12 months. For investors starting out, with the intention of buying a single property or a small number of properties, this structure can be an effective and logical choice.

Family trusts

A family trust is a common entity used to buy property by investors with larger portfolios. A family trust is also called a *discretionary trust*, because the *trustee* (responsible for the trust) has the discretion to allocate income to different beneficiaries (people or entities who benefit from the income generated by the trust's assets).

At the end of each tax year, the trust must distribute (allocate) the income generated by its assets to the beneficiaries and this income is then assessed with the beneficiary's other net income for tax purposes. If a trust doesn't distribute income earned for some reason there can be tax rate penalties. The trust itself doesn't pay the tax, the beneficiaries do (on profits that are distributed to them from the trust). Obviously, if no profit is made, no distribution is paid!

There are potential tax benefits from holding property in a family trust, as income generated from rent or selling can be allocated to beneficiaries with the best tax position, legally reducing the tax that is paid on income produced by assets the trust holds. There are also asset protection benefits as property is held 'in trust' so it cannot be easily accessed in the event that someone wishes to sue you personally.

There are set-up costs for a trust (several thousand dollars) and annual costs for preparing tax returns. Generally, property held in a trust should be positively or neutrally geared because losses made by the property won't offset any income for tax purposes.

For investors with firm plans to build a longer-term, multi-property portfolio in the near future, this structure may be something worth discussing with an experienced property accountant.

Note: there are other kinds of trusts that we won't go into here for simplicity.

Partnerships

A partnership is a situation where multiple individuals work together towards a common goal. Legally, a partnership can be formed where documentation describes the means in which these individuals are working together and an agreement is drafted and executed. A partnership is a legally-recognised arrangement, governed by state law.

In a legal partnership, both (or all) partners have "joint and several liability" which means that each partner is responsible and liable for the debts of not only their share but the entire partnership. Property can be bought in a partnership of multiple individuals, a partnership of multiple trusts, companies, etc.

It may be easier for a partnership to secure finance as lenders will look at all parties when assessing loans. There are set-up and annual costs when you choose this structure which include legal fees and costs for preparing tax returns.

A partnership should not be entered into lightly. It is extremely important, if you do choose this structure, to draft a "dissolution agreement" that clearly states what will happen when a partnership breaks down and/or is wound up. Also it needs to be discussed and documented what will happen in the event that things don't go to plan, including if the partnership makes a loss or needs extra cash, etc.

Generally, all partnerships will end (hopefully amicably) as a partnership is formed with a specific goal in mind. Once the goal is reached, or when one or both of the partners is no longer seeking the same goal, the decision will be made for the partnership to be discontinued. Depending on what assets are held by the partnership, and how these are to be distributed upon dissolution, it might take considerable time for the partnership to end (e.g. several years is common).

Partnerships can be a very good way for investors who are starting out to leverage and reach goals faster and they are also a very good learning experience for business people. If you are interested in pursuing a partnership, consider further research, and also check out **www.achieveproperty/partnerships**.

Companies

A company is a legal entity that can acquire property. Benefits to companies are that the tax that a company pays is fixed (currently at 30% at time of writing), and companies have limited liability for shareholders. Companies are not eligible for a capital gains discount, so care needs to be taken when buying in a company structure if you intend to sell a property for capital gains after 12 months (as you may pay more tax than if you bought in a different structure).

In many cases, an investor may use a family trust with a corporate trustee. This is a situation where the company is responsible for the running of the trust. The director of the company is responsible for the company and indirectly, therefore, for the running of the trust. The director of the company and the beneficiary of the trust may be the same person.

Your accountant can advise if this is an appropriate structure for your investing (especially if you are considering using a family trust) as there may be asset protection advantages in this set-up too.

Self managed superannuation funds (SMSFs)

Currently, there is a lot of information around about buying property through a self managed super fund.

Over the last decade, partially due to huge falls in superannuation balances during the GFC, there have been thousands more people deciding to manage their own retirement savings and start their own SMSF. Currently, more than one million people in Australia are members of an SMSF and collectively SMSFs manage about one-third of Australia's $1.4 trillion superannuation savings. Not all of these funds are buying property but they can if they want to.

A self managed super fund is a trust structure. There is flexibility in the number of people who can belong to a single SMSF – anything from an individual to a group of four people, though they must be related to you. Having more people in an SMSF means they can pool their cash and buy more, however they would ideally want to have the same investment outcomes in mind. Super really is a long-term investment. Set-up costs are quite reasonable but compliance is stringent and penalties for non-compliance are harsh. Superannuation is concessionally-taxed and managing your own super can give you more flexibility and wider investment options. It used to be recommended that people need at least $200,000 in super savings to manage their own fund, however it can be done with less. For advice speak to your accountant, financial planner or other financial advisers.

Recently laws have been changed and self managed super funds can borrow money which allows them to leverage to buy bigger properties. The rules around borrowing to invest in property through an SMSF are quite complex and lenders are more conservative, generally offering lower LVRs.

Property developers and salespeople have realised that superannuation is a relatively untapped source of funds and some encourage investors to consider setting up their own fund with the express purpose of borrowing to invest in their property. While investing to purchase property through an SMSF is not necessarily a bad thing, it should be approached with caution. If you are considering this approach, be sure to seek specialist advice. For people looking to invest directly in property using their super, an SMSF is the only option and may be the way to go.

If you are interested in investing in property using superannuation, check out **www.achieveproperty.com/superannuation**.

Consulting your solicitor

When you have decided in what structure you will be making your property investment, you need to talk to your solicitor about drafting the contract in this name – or at least ensuring that the correct details are filled in. It is not easy to change the ownership entity once the property has been settled and can be difficult or costly even just once the final contracts have exchanged. In some cases you would need to physically sell the property and realise any capital gains and re-purchase in the new entity's name (for example if you bought through a partnership and wanted to take over sole-ownership in your own name, or if you bought in your own name and wanted instead to use a trust structure). This could mean you would have to pay all conveyancing costs – including a hefty stamp duty bill, just to re-structure. When starting out, often it's easier to just sell in this situation but it's nice to have thought about this before and save the hassle of needing to re-think structuring down the track.

If you are thinking of using any structure other than your own name, then start talking to your solicitor early in the piece. It can take considerable time to set up a structure (this will vary depending on which you use) but you don't want this to delay your purchase.

Having a good solicitor experienced in property investing and structuring is essential when you start to build your property portfolio.

The next step in structuring

Given the complexity of this topic, and because taxation and company rules constantly change, it is really important to speak to an adviser (usually your accountant) regarding the best structure for your investing.

For information on legal and accounting advisers, go to **www.achieveproperty.com/advisors**.

CHAPTER SUMMARY

- Structuring refers to the entity that you purchase your property in.
- Tax implications, asset protection and cost of set-up and running the entity are factors that will need to be taken into consideration when deciding how to structure your portfolio.
- Common structures include:
  - Ownership in own name
  - Family trust
  - Partnership
  - Company
  - Combinations/variations of the above
  - Self managed superannuation funds.

Talk to your property investing accountant and solicitor about the right structure for your portfolio.

Links

For further information about legal and professional advisers, accountants, solicitors, you can visit:
www.achieveproperty.com/advisors.

Information on Partnerships
www.achieveproperty/partnerships

Information on self-managed super funds (SMSFs) and buying investment property with super
www.achieveproperty.com/superannuation

CHAPTER NOTES AND ACTIONS

Before moving on to the next chapter, spend a few minutes writing down the things that resonated with you from this chapter.

What actions do you need to take, or what do you need to plan to do, to help you get to the next level in your investing?

Write down at least 5 things now.

1. _____

2. _____

3. _____

4. _____

5. _____

16

ACCOUNTING, BOOK-KEEPING AND TAX

- *Good record-keeping and book-keeping will save you time and money in the long run*
- *Taxation is not all about paying tax, there are deductions you can claim too*
- *You need to select a team of professionals with expertise in these areas to help you.*

When you are just starting to invest in property, there is a lot to learn and so many vital things to focus on. In the scheme of things, book-keeping, accounting and tax may seem a bit less important (at least initially). I completely agree. There is no point getting bogged down in any of these things when buying your first property or properties. What is important is to get started and buy the best property you can, with your current level of knowledge. The intricacies of tax and accounting can be learned as you go and handled predominantly by professionals in those areas.

However, if you take a couple of small things into consideration, it can make your foray into property investing a lot easier and set you up for ongoing success as you look to grow your portfolio into the future. Doing these things the wrong way may mean delays and losses.

Accounting

In Australia, tax law is quite complex. As we have covered in the previous chapter, there are various structures that you can use to buy property in, and even if you buy in your own name, there are deductions, depreciations, taxes, grants, and tax discounts that all may vary depending on the structure, the property, and the state you invest in.

Firstly, don't get bogged down by these and don't feel that you need to know everything before you get started. You can get advice on most of these things as you go, and you can certainly learn as you go. It is really important to have a good property accountant who can give you advice on what to do when it comes to structuring and other questions.

For some recommendations on property accountants, see **www.achieveproperty.com/advisors**.

Book-keeping

When starting out, you probably don't need a book-keeper just yet. A book-keeper is someone who records all your income and expenses, and your assets and liabilities (keeping track of your properties and mortgages). However, as you grow your portfolio, a book-keeper is highly recommended. This task is time-consuming and it is better to pay someone to manage your books than try to do it all yourself to save money – allow yourself the time to find more property deals instead. This is especially important for those of us who are investing in our spare time, because this is a limited resource we need to optimise!

It is a good idea to start creating good book-keeping habits from the start, however.

Good book-keeping and accounting habits

You should have an in-tray for all expenses relating to your property investing activities and these should be reviewed weekly and paid when they are due. Expenses include council rates, water rates, insurance, property management expenses, bank statements, etc. When your mail arrives, add the new expense invoice to the tray chronologically in order of date due for payment.

Spare time investors need to prioritise book-keeping tasks and be disciplined in attending to them. Schedule some time one evening a week, or a weekend (or a week day if you have time on a day during the week) to pay all your expenses. Paying weekly means this becomes a routine and won't be forgotten! Once the expense is paid, file the invoice away – either in a folder/ filing cabinet, or scan it and file it electronically (remember, it is vital to keep backups of electronic data).

Personally, I file away all my invoices manually, and also submit them electronically to my book-keeper via drop-box. This is an efficient way of transporting files relatively securely and means that we can both maintain this system.

For manual filing, I recommend one folder for each property. I use different coloured manila folders, with the name of the property written on the top of each folder. I use a filing cabinet, but a bookshelf or box would be fine so long as the paperwork won't fall out.

Inside each folder, are the following sections:

1. Income
2. Landlording expenses
3. Insurance
4. Building expenses
5. Building documents
6. Property purchasing – due diligence
7. Property purchasing – legal
8. Property purchasing – costs
9. Finance.

I identify each section with a sticky note on the front of the collection of invoices, and use a paperclip to hold all related invoices together. The simpler your system, the better.

When you are buying a property, you will be mostly filing paperwork in sections #6, #7, #8, and #9. Once you are holding the property, most of your filing will be in sections #1 and #2, but some repairs or renovations may be filed in #4 and #5. Income is at the front, as it is the most important!

If you file things away either when you pay the invoice, or once a month, then your book-keeping will always be kept under control. Should you choose to file monthly, then have another folder where you keep your invoices that have been paid but not properly filed yet.

One reason it is important to have a good filing system is that, as your portfolio grows and you are seeking more finance, your financier will want to see copies of your income statements and mortgage statements in your future finance applications. When you want to submit a finance application, you don't want to have to spend too much time looking for documents.

Book-keeping software

While there are many options available for managing your property's books, I only recommend two options.

If you are starting out and have one or two properties, then the easiest solution is to manually track your finances with a spreadsheet such as Excel (Microsoft) or Numbers (Mac). Record all income and expenses on a monthly basis, starting from the beginning of the financial year. At the end of the year, add up all your income and expenses and submit these to your accountant (they can advise on and calculate any depreciation or other deductions).

BONUS: You can download a ready-made spreadsheet from our bonus tools section at www.achieveproperty.com/bonustools.

If you elect to track your income and expenses with a proper accounting program, rather than a spreadsheet, I recommend you use MYOB (Mind Your Own Business) business software. This software may be a bit more complicated than others on the market, however it is real accounting software and will be easier for your book-keeper and accountant to use as your portfolio grows.

Getting used to MYOB will also help you understand some of the important accounting principles of growing a business. Furthermore, the reports that can be generated by the software will be invaluable as you track your portfolio's growth and you need to provide statements for financiers down the track. You only need the basic accounting package which will probably cost a couple of hundred dollars and is a very worthwhile investment to make. There are new versions of this software coming out all the time, and currently my book-keeper and I are trialling a new cloud-based solution that looks really cool.

Tax

There are many aspects of tax that you will learn as you grow your property portfolio. This is something else not to get too bogged down with at the start.

An important principle to remember is that *you will pay tax when you make money*, after all, taxes are an important part of our society and everyone needs to contribute. Your aim in investing is to pay the minimum tax you legally need to, and more importantly, to focus on *making money*, not just saving tax.

Taxation is not just about paying tax, there are taxation allowances that property investors can claim such as depreciation on their property. Depending on how your investment is structured, you may also be able to offset tax payable with any losses you have made (although, as I said earlier, your intention should always be to make a profit).

Depreciation

As we briefly touched on before, depreciation is a much overlooked part of accounting for property investors, and can be an important way to improve your portfolio's overall and short-term cash flow.

Depreciation is a great way of reducing tax in the short-term because by depreciating materials in your properties (claiming a tax offset for things you own that have gone down in value over time), you can increase your cash flow. You can then invest this money instead of paying it to the government, and get better returns this way.

What is important when looking at depreciation is that you don't try to justify buying a negatively-geared property as 'positive' cash flow just because you can depreciate assets. Especially if your intention is to sell that asset, some of the depreciation you may have claimed on the building costs will be added to the cost base when you sell, so you do pay this back (it will reduce the amount of profit at the end, because your capital gains tax will go up).

Some sellers of property will somewhat misleadingly advertise property as positive cash flow, only because once depreciation is taken into consideration you may save tax and be able to get some cash flow back when you do your tax return. This will be dependent on the structure you buy in as well – so you may not be eligible in any case.

To summarise, every investor should talk to their accountant about depreciation and consider this as part of their overall investing strategy if appropriate.

Capital gains and losses

When you sell property, you will generally make a profit (hopefully) or a loss (maybe sometimes). A profit will mean that you've sold for more than you bought and still have money left over when also taking into consideration all the costs of buying, holding and selling your property. This 'profit' is referred to as a 'capital gain' – because you have 'gained' capital (a financial resource available for use). If you end up with less money at the end, this is a 'capital loss'.

Even if you don't sell, your property can increase in value, and you can refinance against this unrealised (unsold) capital gain and then draw down on the equity (additional value) to use as a deposit for additional loans, etc.

It is important when looking at the numbers of a property deal to include all the costs that you incur at purchase, and during the holding period of the property, and at sale. These numbers need to be considered in your calculations with regard to profitability of any property you buy. This is because you could in theory sell for more than you bought, but still make a loss if your costs incurred between buying and selling are too high. For example, many first-time investors make the mistake of over-capitalising on a renovation (spending too much) then find that they cannot sell for a high enough price to make up the difference. As a result, they don't achieve a profit, they end up making a capital loss.

Operating expenses versus capital expenses

Without going into too much detail about accounting, the expenses that you incur can be categorised into two main types:

- operating expenses
- capital expenses.

The reason you want to have an understanding of this is because these are treated differently when it comes to tax, book-keeping and accounting.

Operating expenses are the costs you incur to hold a property (e.g. management, some maintenance and interest costs, costs of driving to and from a rental property after you've bought it, etc.). These expenses are *immediately* deductible against the income your property generates, so these will reduce the tax you pay at the end of the year.

Capital expenses are the costs you incur when adding value to a property (e.g. most renovating costs, some buying expenses like stamp duty, legal fees on purchase, etc.). These amounts are not tax deductible at the end of the financial year, but will be taken into consideration to offset capital gains tax when you sell.

If you are not sure how to categorise an expense, your accountant or book-keeper can tell you which costs belong to which category and they will classify the costs of your investing into one of these two areas. Your accountant will let you know what the tax implications are of your investing.

Capital gains tax (CGT)

In most cases investment properties will attract capital gains tax which you pay after selling (provided you make a profit). If you make a loss, then this loss can usually be carried forward to offset tax you pay when you make a profit at a later date.

One of the really great things about property investing and capital gains, is that *you only pay capital gains tax when you sell*. Unlike working in a job, where you get taxed every month, your property portfolio can keep growing in value and you can delay paying tax year after year, if you hold and just don't sell. This is not a reason to never sell. But it is a great way to improve your financial situation without needing to worry about tax in the short term. If you hold your property deal for more than 12 months, then in most cases you will be entitled to the CGT discount which means you only pay CGT on 50% of your profit.

Land tax

In some cases there may be land tax to pay but this is usually a small amount of money paid annually, and as a rule, land tax isn't something to worry about that would affect your decision to buy a property. However, if you are buying in an area where the value of land is high, (e.g. in the inner city) then the amount of land tax you might pay could be a bit more substantial. Check with your accountant the implications of land tax before you buy if you are worried. Generally I just think of land tax as a small but annoying cost of business.

The structure you buy in can affect the tax you will pay

Depending on the structure that you buy in, you may pay more or less tax, so it is worth discussing this with your accountant when setting up your structure. Remember, at the end of the day, no one likes paying tax but paying tax is a good thing because it means you made money!

My advice is to not let the accounting side of things worry you too much, especially when you are starting, because you can leave this to your advisers – that is what they are for.

Once you gain some experience, if you want to know more about this stuff, read a book like *Accounting for Dummies* and it will start to make a bit more sense.

Getting professional help

Your accountant is your best adviser when it comes to tax, as accountants learn the latest rulings and their job is to prepare your tax returns so that you won't get audited (or, if the tax department does audit you, that it is not a painful process). However, if your accountant is adamant that negative gearing is the only kind of investing, then consider a different accountant.

CHAPTER SUMMARY

- Accounting, book-keeping and tax can seem daunting, but for a beginner investor, while it is important to know about these, you should not need to be overly concerned about them – this is what your expert team is for.
- It is worth starting with good habits that will serve you over your investing career, so get used to tracking income and expenses, either using a spreadsheet such as Microsoft Excel or Numbers on the Mac, or using accounting software such as MYOB.
- Know what 'capital gains' means and be aware of the difference between capital expenses and operating expenses.
- Operating expenses are immediately deductible and capital expenses will offset the capital gains you pay when you sell.
- Be aware that the structure you buy in can affect the tax you will pay in the future.
- Be sure to ask your accountant for advice and for explanations if you have any questions.

Links

For more information about legal and professional advisers, accountants, solicitors
www.achieveproperty.com/advisors

Download a ready-made spreadsheet from our bonus tools section at www.achieveproperty.com/bonustools.

Accounting, book-keeping and tax

CHAPTER NOTES AND ACTIONS

Before moving on to the next chapter, spend a few minutes writing down the things that resonated with you from this chapter.

What actions do you need to take, or what do you need to plan to do, to help you get to the next level in your investing?

Write down at least 5 things now.

1. _____

   _____

   _____

2. _____

   _____

   _____

3. _____

   _____

   _____

4. _____

   _____

   _____

5. _____

   _____

   _____

17

LEARNING THE TECHNIQUES TO INVEST IN PROPERTY

- *Investing in property investment education is an important step*
- *Successful investors develop a property investing mindset*
- *There is a range of education available, but be selective.*

Our aim at the beginning of the book was to convince would-be investors that property investing can be started and done successfully in your spare time. The first thing to do is to work out what's stopping you and we have addressed each limiting factor up to this point in the book.

We have covered a lot of content so far – from how to find money to start investing, how to get finance, how interest rates and property prices work, how to be an effective landlord, making money from investing and what property to look for, as well as information on accounting and book-keeping.

Now that we have all this information we can use it to find and buy our first investment property. In this final chapter, we are going to list, step-by-step, what we need to do to buy and manage our first investment property.

But before we do, let's have a look at some more advanced techniques in property investing and how to develop the right mindset. How do we fast-track our education and where are the best places to learn more?

When I started investing, education systems, knowledge sources and property mentoring programs were in their infancy in Australia. A lot has happened since then, with a range of programs emerging from the property boom of the late 1990s and early 2000s. Many books have been written and many courses have been developed. Not all of these are of the same standard, but finding the right courses will propel you forward in your investing journey (provided you take action). The wrong courses will cost you money and time. So where do you start?

I have invested heavily in my property education over a number of years and, as a result, have made returns of many times the amount spent. I don't necessarily recommend jumping in and immediately doing the same – at least not initially. But when you are ready to go further in your investing, it might be time to consider further education.

What property investing education is available?

There are several kinds of courses available, let's look at these and where you might want to start, depending on your goals. My advice when deciding on how to educate yourself, is to work out what you are trying to achieve (your goals) then work backwards to decide what courses you want to attend. As there are many choices, it is easy to sign up for lots of information and not necessarily use any of it. The important thing is to seek education then take action.

I would categorise property investing courses into three main types (though there is some cross-over).

1. Specific property investing technique education
2. General/thorough property investing education systems
3. Property investing mentoring.

Property investing technique education

Specific property investing technique education aims to teach a selective skill or educate you on one type of deal. For example, popular areas of education include 'vendor finance' (commonly referred to as 'no money down investing' or 'buy a house for $1'), property options, property developing, negotiation skills, etc. These courses are useful if you have identified an area you want to move into and require some specific training or you need to develop a new skill, or improve your ability in a skill you have started to learn.

General property investing education

General property investing education systems might cover a large range of property investing techniques, but to less of a degree than the specific courses. These courses might be more useful for people starting out who don't yet know specifically what techniques they want to use, or who are looking at developing a range of techniques that they can use depending on the situation.

Depending on where you are at in your investing, either or both of these types of courses might suit you.

Property investing mentoring

The last area of education is property investing mentoring. Often this may be included alongside or after a specific or general education course. Mentoring involves regular contact with a more experienced investor who can provide insight and guide a less-experienced investor through their property deals.

The advantage of mentoring is that costly mistakes can hopefully be avoided and progress is made faster, as the mentor has travelled the path already and can point the student in the right direction. A good mentor allows their student to solve their problems themselves, but in a positive and cost-effective and timely manner. All successful experienced investors have had (or in most cases still do have) mentors.

As property investing courses are constantly being introduced and changed, we won't cover specific courses in this book, but you can see our website **www.achieveproperty.com/education** for more specific information and links to courses that are available from a range of educators.

Learning strategies and resources

People who are most successful in learning a new skill (including property investing) are able to become focused on learning the techniques required. Science shows us that we learn far more effectively when we focus, rather than when we try to multi-task. So if you are not absorbing the information you are exposing yourself to consider whether you are distracted or not fully committed to your education. If you struggle to find time for education, consider listening to audiobooks or MP3s as you drive to and from work (or if you catch the train, even better). Most people have at least a 30 minute commute to work, and this is a great time to listen to educational material. The benefit of regular (e.g. daily) consistent education is that you start to develop your mindset which will lead to success.

If you are not yet ready to invest in a full education program, or mentoring, there are plenty of places to gather useful information at a fraction of the cost. Property magazine subscriptions, books and audio programs are highly recommended (either alone, or in adjunct with other materials) to accelerate your learning.

Alternatively, free options for starting your education include books from the library, videos from YouTube, property forums on the internet, (free) property seminars, and networking with experienced investors who are usually more than happy to share stories, offer advice and inspiration. Keep in mind that the quality of free material varies, and the latest techniques may not be available from your library.

Visit **www.achieveproperty.com/recommendedresources** for a list of recommended books and free resources.

For most people it's not a lack of knowledge that holds them back, but a lack of action. If you have spent fifty dollars, several hundred dollars, or several thousand dollars on education, you are more likely to put in the action to see your education pay off. It is for this reason that I recommend paying money for quality education, and then taking the action to see significant returns on your financial investment. If $1,000+ has been committed to education, you might be more inclined to do the work and take the action to get the results. Don't be afraid to spend money on your education.

Developing the right mindset

One of the most important aspects to getting started in property investing, and then going on to succeed, is development of the mindset of a successful property investor. Very few people actually achieve this, which is why even though so many people start getting educated, there are relatively few truly successful investors. In essence if you want to be a successful investor, you need to think like a real investor. The best way to achieve this is two-fold:

1. Firstly, learn the mindset from a property-investing simulation game
2. Secondly, start investing in real life.

Learning the techniques to invest in property

Property investing simulation games

The best way to learn the mindset using a property-investing simulation game is to play Cashflow®, a game invented by Robert Kiyosaki (a property and wealth creation pioneer and best-selling author of *Rich Dad, Poor Dad*, among other titles).

This game is literally a property-investing and wealth-creation simulator for training property investors. I recommend ALL upcoming investors use this game for their education, before buying in the real world, in much the same way that pilots learn on a flight simulator before they are allowed to fly in the real world. After all, when the thing you are driving is worth hundreds of thousands of dollars, you don't want it to come crashing down around you, do you?

While you can play Cashflow® with your friends and family, or online, I highly recommend playing the game with experienced investors who are passionate about you learning the right way. For information on recommended groups to join to play Cashflow®, check out **www.achieveproperty.com/cashflow**. Participating in this activity is a very cost-effective way to develop the right mindset to become a successful investor. You should play Cashflow® monthly (or at any opportunity) as you work on developing your mindset for successful investing.

Attending seminars

The other strong recommendation for investors who are starting out, is to attend regular seminars on property investing, to hear about different techniques and success stories of people who are investing in the current market. This will help you realise that it is possible for you to do the same, and sooner than you think! On top of this, seminars are a great place to meet like-minded investors, and you should always exchange details, as you never know who might be your next JV partner, money partner, or who might give you an idea for your next property deal.

Visit **www.achieveproperty.com/propertymeetings** for recommended property meetings.

The aim of immersing yourself in investment books, courses, seminars, simulators, discussions and audio recordings is to develop the mindset of an investor – that is, to start thinking like a property investor. If you can do this, you are on your way to investing success.

CHAPTER SUMMARY

- As you progress in your investing, you will probably want to seek out more education. Most people don't yet know enough to be successful when they are just starting out. Education can help hasten the process of progressing as an investor.
- Educational programs will provide:
  - Specific property investing technique education
  - General/thorough property investing education systems
  - Property investing mentoring
- In deciding what courses you need to do, work out your long-term goals, then work backwards, scheduling the training you require as you progress.
- Choose your next education based on the gaps in your knowledge or confidence.
- There are plenty of free seminars available if you aren't ready to pay for your education (though many of these will be precursors to selling a bigger course).
- It is essential to develop the mindset of an investor if you wish to be successful. To help with this, attend regular (monthly) Cashflow® events and property investing meetings.

Links

For more information about property investing courses available from a range of educators, visit:
www.achieveproperty.com/education

Free books and resources are listed at:
www.achieveproperty.com/recommendedresources

Details of Cashflow® events can be found at:
www.achieveproperty.com/cashflow

For information about property meetings visit:
www.achieveproperty.com/propertymeetings.

CHAPTER NOTES AND ACTIONS

Before moving on to the next chapter, spend a few minutes writing down the things that resonated with you from this chapter.

What actions do you need to take, or what do you need to plan to do, to help you get to the next level in your investing?

Write down at least 5 things now.

1. _____

_____

_____

2. _____

_____

_____

3. _____

_____

_____

4. _____

_____

_____

5. _____

_____

_____

18

BUYING YOUR FIRST INVESTMENT PROPERTY – STEP-BY-STEP

- *It is essential to support your investing with ongoing education*
- *By following this investment process you will successfully buy your first investment property*
- *You will need to check legislation in the state where you are buying.*

This final chapter is dedicated to helping you buy your first investment property. You really need to have read the preceding 17 chapters before you go through this step-by-step process. So if you have cheated and skipped ahead you may need to go back!

We will break the steps down into three sections:

1. Things you should be doing regularly
2. Further education to consider (if you feel you need it)
3. Step-by-step buying your first investment property

1. Things you should be doing regularly:

- Reading property investing books, listening to audios
  www.achieveproperty.com/recommendedresources
- Attending Cashflow® events, monthly
  www.achieveproperty.com/cashflow
- Attending property investing meetings
  www.achieveproperty.com/propertymeetings

Maintain these activities and you will develop the mindset of an investor.

2. **For further education, consider:**
   - General property investing education
   - Specific property investing education
   - Property investing mentoring.

If you are looking for more skills, or want greater confidence before launching into buying a property, these are the recommended areas to look for further education. When you are ready, proceed to #3 and let's get started on buying your first (or subsequent) investment property!

3. **Buying your first investment property**

Congratulations on making it to here. Buying your first investment property is an exciting and scary time. The aim of this section is to give you some of the insights into the process you need to go through to buy an investment property. Because the goal is to buy a property, we have deliberately kept this section simple, so as not to overwhelm the reader. However, if you feel that you need more information, you should seek professional advice (from your accountant or solicitor) or a mentor.

This process is likely to take at least a couple of months from the start even just through to the negotiation stage. So don't feel frustrated, or that things are moving too slowly, if you are taking your time. After all, buying a house is a major investment.

The guidelines below outline the process for buying property using Australia as an example (and more specifically New South Wales). However, if you are buying anywhere else, don't let this put you off! The same principles apply in NSW as in other states of Australia and all over the world. Some of the specifics are a little different (often easier!), and the best people to get advice from are your solicitor, finance broker and accountant. Don't be afraid to ask them to clearly explain the process involved – that is what you are paying them for. So if you are investing somewhere else, approach your advisers, and ask them to outline the process in your area – particularly for Steps #6 to #9, #11 and #13.

STEP #1 – Identify what you want to buy

Go back to Chapter Twelve and work through the steps again in the first part of this chapter to identify the kind of property that you want, and the area you want to look at. Keep in mind the things discussed in Chapter Eleven and how you might add value to the property.

STEP #2 – Search for properties in your area that fit your criteria

Having decided what you want to buy, down to as much detail as you can, jump online on **www.realestate.com.au** or **www.domain.com.au** or other property sale websites, and see if you can find property that suit your criteria. Confirm that you can buy property for the price you want and that after value-adding (to hold, or sell) that your property will be worth what you want. Also establish that the property will rent for the yield that you require. If you wish, you can physically visit the area at this time, inspect properties, drive the streets, take notes. If the area is not geographically close, then you can virtually do the same using Google Street-view. But you will need to physically get there in Step #Five.

STEP #3 – Assemble your team of professionals

Having established that you have an area where properties meet your criteria, it is time to interview your team of professionals. Line up meetings with the people you will need to close the deal.

At this stage, you will want to engage a solicitor or conveyancer, as well as a finance broker. You may want to speak to an accountant as well – this is recommended, but if you don't yet have a good property accountant, don't let this hold you back. Remember, if you are looking for a team of professionals, check out **www.achieveproperty.com/advisors.**

The reason to do this now is that when you find a property to buy, things start to move quickly and you want to already know who your team is. You will need to provide the selling agent with the name and contact details of your solicitor, so if you already know this, it's less stressful and you will look more professional.

You will also want to speak to your finance broker, at this stage, to get an idea of your borrowing capacity and which lenders and what lending products you will consider for your first purchase. Your broker will ask you for details on your income and expenses and from this give you an idea of how much you can borrow. They will let you know the likely interest rate you will borrow at and you can use this in your calculations when assessing property that you look at.

If you are buying in your own name then there is nothing more to do here. For most first-time investors this may be the easiest option. If you are using a different entity or structure then speak to your accountant about this and about setting up a structure if you haven't already done this.

STEP #4 – *Educate yourself on the values of properties in your area*

Now go back to Chapter Nine and review the section on property valuation. You have an idea that the property you are buying is going to be a certain price, and that it will sell at a certain price once renovated (or once another value-adding technique has been applied). However, you need to be certain. Advertised prices for properties, as a rule, may be 10% above what the vendor will accept. Use valuation software to get a good idea of the median price in the area where you are looking and determine how prices are trending. Depending on the software you choose to use, you can possibly get a lot more useful information on your specific property as well.

Don't forget to check out **www.achieveproperty.com/valuation**.

Download a map of the area and find out how much houses sell for, and rent for, in different parts of the area. What is the 'good' part and what is the 'bad' part of town? Are there housing commission areas? It might be recommended to avoid these.

At the same time, speak to locals and agents about developments in the area, new infrastructure, new businesses, new shops or services. Try to establish if there is likely to be economic growth in the near future that may mean more money being spent locally (therefore stimulating the local economy leading to potentially increased house prices).

Remember you are looking for a property that is quality (even if it might need work) but is selling for low-market value. You need to distinguish this from a cheap property that is selling at-market value because that is what it is worth.

STEP #5 – Find a good deal

Having done this work, it is now time to start looking for your property deal. You might have come across a deal already in your previous investigations. It is interesting how often the first property you come across (or the last) might just happen to be the one you buy.

Re-read the middle and last sections in Chapter Twelve and use the tools suggested at **www.achieveproperty.com/searchtools** if you need to.

Look for property that fit the criterion that price isn't as important to the vendor as something else you can offer them (e.g. a quick sale or terms that the vendor will value).

You MUST visit the property in person at this stage. As an investor who is starting out it is imperative that you drive (or walk) around the area and become familiar with properties. If the area you are buying in is regional then spend at least a full weekend inspecting as many properties as you can. Better to spend a couple of weekends so that you can revisit with fresh eyes after your initial inspection to make an educated decision as to whether this is the right place for your first purchase.

Look for a property that is of good structural quality. Not being a builder, you will have a building inspection done, but it's worth looking thoroughly through the property yourself – don't waste money on a building inspection on a property that you can tell yourself is falling down.

When you do inspect properties you are interested in, take a clipboard and paper, and make notes of everything that might need repair – or things that can be renovated to add value. If nothing else, this gives the impression that you are a seasoned investor and you know how much it is worth so that you won't be pushed on price.

Sloping floors are generally an indication that piers (stumps) need to be fixed (raised or replaced). Significant slope may indicate other issues. Doors that don't close or open may also be an indication of other problems. Old hot water systems (greater than 15 years old) may need replacing soon and this may be a cost. Your building inspection will turn up things you need to know about, so don't get overwhelmed during your first inspection.

Once you have seen enough properties, and found the best one, you can make an offer!

Before you do make an offer, ask the agent to email you a copy of the contract and ask them what the market rent for the property will be. Ensure the rent will provide a yield acceptable to you from this investment.

You'll want the contract later and asking for it also makes you look more professional (as if you need to review the contract before you can think about making an offer). If you have a mentor, or an experienced investor you can talk to, go through the contract with them. If not, don't worry too much, your solicitor will look at this in more detail later.

STEP #6 – Negotiate a price and have the offer accepted

Negotiating is a skill that you will learn as you progress as an investor. The best way to learn is to make lots of offers (and why not buy lots of property at the same time!). But let's start with one property first. When it comes to negotiating, there are entire books and courses dedicated to this subject. If you aren't yet comfortable with negotiating, then read a book, or do a course. Alternatively, find a mentor and have them guide you through the process. Some options are available at **www.achieveproperty.com/education**.

Having already reviewed the information in the second section of Chapter Twelve, try to make an offer that suits the vendor's needs in order to create a win-win situation. For example, this might be a situation where you benefit from the price and they benefit from the terms.

You can download the bonus report "20 Rules for Successful Offers" now from **www.achieveproperty.com/bonus-tools**.

Your offer should always be in writing (but when counter-offering, email may be OK depending on the situation). In some states of Australia, your offer is made in writing and contracts are exchanged at the time the offer is accepted. In other states, the acceptance of the offer and the exchange of contracts occur as two separate events. Speak to your solicitor or mentor about the process in the state where you are purchasing.

It is highly recommended to give a small goodwill holding deposit at the time of offer acceptance. Often real estate agents refuse this at first but I generally push the point – as this shows you are serious about buying the property and, in states where you have not yet exchanged contracts, this helps reduce the risk of gazumping (where someone buys the property from under you, before you have exchanged contracts). Always have a clause in your offer that should your due diligence not pass your standards the goodwill holding deposit will be refunded immediately. The deposit should be paid to the selling agent's trust account. The amount paid is usually $1,000, regardless of the value of the property.

Finally, always have a get-out clause in your offer and/or contract if necessary (depending on whether you exchange contracts at offer acceptance or later). Your get-out clause should enable you to pull out for any reason you are not happy but should be phrased in such a way that it doesn't sound as if you will. A useful clause to use is outlined in the bonus report. If you have any questions speak to your solicitor.

Once your offer is accepted – congratulations!

Ask the selling agent to send you a quick email, advising in writing that your offer has been accepted. Also, ask the agent for their trust account details, so you can direct-deposit your $1,000 goodwill holding deposit (if this was in your offer). You should then request that the property manager provide a letter estimating the market rent for the property. Lastly, provide the agent with your solicitor's contact details.

Celebrate, then contact your solicitor and let them know your offer was accepted. Over the next few days the selling agent will issue a notice of sale and then they will contact your solicitor with details you provide them.

STEP #7 – Full due diligence

Before we get started on due diligence, now is the time to organise your filing system. Don't worry – we will keep this simple.

Re-read Chapter Sixteen and the section of the chapter "Good book-keeping and accounting habits". Create a folder as suggested. You will file all your due diligence reports under the section in the folder: "Property purchasing due diligence". You are probably going to create an electronic folder on your computer for your property too so feel free to replicate the same folders here. When you get a copy of the contract, and any communications from your solicitor, file these under "Property purchasing – legal". This way, you will always be able to find what you are looking for. Within each section, filing in chronological order is best, from oldest at the front, to newest at the back, each section secured by a paperclip.

OK, now we are organised, let's get on with the due diligence.

Re-read Chapter Thirteen and follow each due diligence step outlined. Keep notes in the electronic folder on your computer and the manual file you just created. Also look at Step #Eight below. Steps #Seven and #Eight are done simultaneously, don't wait until you finish Step #Seven to start Step #Eight.

When you are happy that your due diligence has been completed, you are a step closer to unconditional exchange.

STEP #8 – Have finance approved

Having already met with your broker, and with the knowledge that you should be able to get finance approval for your purchase, now is the time to get finance actually approved. Contact your broker again and let them know the exciting news that your offer has been accepted.

Email your broker:

1. A copy of the first two pages of the contract
2. A letter from a property manager demonstrating the market rent for the property
3. The address of the property (it will be on the contract anyway)
4. The purchase price (also on the contract)
5. The LVR you are seeking (refer to Chapter Four if you have forgotten what LVR means)
6. The entity that you will be buying in (if it's not your own name).

The contract will need to have the price filled in plus your details, and your solicitors' details. Either you can wait for the agent to provide this, or you can fill in these details, but don't sign it. This copy of the contract will be needed by your lender (or financier) when they assess you for finance. The financier will also need to see the letter demonstrating market rent for their assessment as well.

If this is the first loan that your broker has done for you, they will likely ask you to fill in some forms. Read through Chapter Five again and be sure to fill in all application forms thoroughly the first time. Provide all documentation that has been asked for (e.g. copies of bank statements, rental statements, etc.).

Ask your broker for an indication of how long it will be until conditional approval is granted. This is where the financier will say you can have the loan, but before they definitely give it to you they will need certain criteria fulfilled, e.g. probably a valuation that they will do on the property.

Also ask your broker when they expect unconditional approval, after this.

Write down these dates and ring the broker a few days before each deadline is due, just to check on how things are progressing. This may help everyone keep their deadlines. In the event of delays, ask what can be done to speed things up, and in particular, what can you do?

Once unconditional approval has been granted IN WRITING you can exchange contracts unconditionally (provided there is nothing else you are waiting for). *Note: Get approval from your advisers – especially your solicitor – before you exchange contracts, see below.*

STEP #9 – Exchange contracts

A week or so before you are due to exchange contracts, you should visit your solicitor, or if you aren't going to see them for a meeting, ask to receive a copy of the final contract by email. Sign the contract and return the physical copy of it to your solicitor. Before signing, be sure that you are completely happy with it, and if you need anything to be explained, now is the time to ask.

Contact the agent and let them know that you are ready to exchange contracts. They will need to receive the deposit amount that is recorded on the contract (usually this is 5% or 10% of the purchase price but it can be any amount), less any goodwill holding deposit you have already given them.

Either provide your solicitor with a cheque, or ask the agent if they would like you to direct deposit the amount into their trust account.

Exchange of contracts will occur between two solicitors' firms, usually offsite somewhere. Your solicitor will let you know when exchange has occurred. Note down the date of exchange of contracts, as settlement will happen a specified number of days following exchange (as outlined in the contract).

Once you have exchanged contracts, you will want to sign your mortgage documents and get these back to the lender as quickly as possible. This will give them the most time available to process your finance in preparation for exchange. Don't be surprised if your lender makes mistakes, this is all too common these days and often results in delays.

Some pages may need to be witnessed by a qualified person (e.g. solicitor, JP or other professional who can be traced, such as a dentist or veterinarian).

> **HOT TIP FOR INVESTORS**
>
> Hint: If you are after a JP to witness a document, many pharmacists will have someone who is qualified in this capacity. They are usually available and generally don't charge for this service.

STEP #10 – Take out insurance

Now is the time to get insurance for your new investment property. Having exchanged contracts, it is worth getting a cover note on the property. In the event that something occurs to the property during the settlement period, should the vendor's insurance not cover it, you could have an issue. Your lender may request a copy of your insurance policy with their details on it, so it is worth getting this ready.

You can either ring around various insurers to get quotes, or you can use an insurance broker to find you the best deal. For first-time investors, landlord insurance that includes rental default is highly recommended, but do the sums and work out for yourself how much cover you want and the cost.

Review Chapter Ten, rule number 2 for more details on

insurance. Visit **www.achieveproperty.com/insurance** for more about insurance brokers.

STEP #11 – Appoint a property manager

As we approach settlement, now is also a good time to interview and appoint a property manager. For the day-to-day running of your portfolio, the property manager is the most important person on your team, after yourself. Many investors fall down by inadequately managing their property manager, or appointing the wrong one.

Review the rest of Chapter Ten and then interview several local property managers in the area of your investment property and appoint one. Often you might end up using the management division of the agency that sells you the property.

If the property is currently vacant, or if the property is lived in by the owner, now is a great time to get a tenant lined up to go in (unless major renovations are needed). If you can have a tenant move in on the day of settlement this will help your cash flow and also maximise the immediate return from the investment. Talk to your property manager about how long they think it will take to rent out the property and see if they have anyone who might be a good candidate already (often they do, especially if the rental market is quite tight).

STEP #12 – Settlement

Forty-two days after exchange of contract (or whatever period was set) settlement will occur.

A week before settlement is due (or maybe a few days) your solicitor will contact you to advise the amount of money needed to finalise settlement. This is called "funds to complete". Generally, the deposit you have given at exchange of contracts is less than the amount you will contribute upon settlement, e.g. you might have a 5% deposit on exchange, but an 80% LVR, meaning you still need to pay 15% of the purchase price, plus any other expenses, to close the sale.

One of the jobs of your solicitor or conveyancer is to liaise with the other side to work out the final cost to each of the vendor and buyer. Once this figure is known, you will be advised how much you need to pay, and you will need to transfer these funds to your solicitor's trust account in advance, so settlement can take place.

Prior to settlement, you need to do a final inspection of the property, or have your agent (e.g. property manager) do an inspection for you.

The aim of this inspection is to ensure that the property is in the condition as specified in the contract and that no damage has occurred during the settlement period, for example while the vendors or tenants were moving out.

If any issues are uncovered during this period, then contact your solicitor immediately and arrange to have these rectified.

> **VERY HOT TIP FOR INVESTORS**
> Hint: Experienced investors can add value to a property during the settlement period and instead of paying money at settlement, they actually receive money. In some cases, for a few thousand dollars of cost, you can add hundreds of thousands in value. I'll cover this in my next book!

Provided that your bank, the vendor, the vendor's bank (if they have a mortgage) and you are all ready, then on settlement day, the property will become yours!

Your bank will create a mortgage and in doing so will use the money they lend you to pay the vendor for the property.

Once the property has settled, the agent will hand over the keys to you or your property manager.

Well done! You just bought your first (or subsequent) investment property! Welcome to property investing.

STEP #13 – Tying up loose ends

I know what you are thinking, "Hang on, I thought we said there were Twelve Steps? What is going on?"

Yes, there are twelve steps to buying a property but the job doesn't finish there. In fact, it's just beginning. And to start with, we need to tie up loose ends.

Your property manager now has the keys to your investment property. If the property is tenanted, and already managed, then you just need to give your contact details and bank details to the property manager, and they will switch across from the previous owner to you. You will get your first statement from them at the end of the month. Find out who is your contact in the managing agency, and keep their details somewhere safe (e.g. on your iPhone contacts list). They will be your first point of contact when you need to talk.

Give them a call and say hi. Check that everything is OK. If your property is vacant, now is the time to get it tenanted.

On the finance side, when your bank created your mortgage, they will have made at least one bank account (the loan account) for you. You should receive notification of this in a couple of days in the mail. The first interest payment won't be due generally until four weeks after settlement. If you haven't received notification in seven days, follow up with your broker and/or the bank.

Once you have your new loan account details, test that your online banking works (try logging into the account). Also check where your interest payment will come from. You might want to go into a local branch for this. If necessary, you can generally change the account that interest is debited from, in the branch. It might make sense to have the same account that rent goes into and interest comes out from.

Your solicitor will send you a statement in a few weeks that details the settlement of the property. This statement (a "Settlement Statement") outlines who paid for what when the property settled.

Water and council rates which are due after settlement but include charges that occurred before, are generally split pro-rata and the vendor and buyer each pay their share. Therefore, the amount that you ended up paying for the property probably is a bit higher or lower when these figures are taken into account.

Keep the Settlement Statement in a safe place (it should be filed in the "Property purchasing – legal" section of your filing folder). This will be needed by your accountant come tax time.

Any immediate post-purchase repairs that are needed should be carried out now. Don't be surprised if there are a few things that turn up that were missed in your initial inspection, e.g. stovetops with one element that doesn't heat up, a toilet that runs constantly, taps that need washers replacing.

If a new tenant will be renting the property, there will usually be minor things that need attention. It is sometimes an idea to let your tenant compile a list of minor issues, then get a handyman to fix everything in one go, rather than sending tradespeople out multiple times.

STEP #14 – Post-purchase management

The rush of buying your property is over.

Unless you are renovating or developing the property, the next process is management, especially if you have purchased a property that is neutral or positive cash flow. Here are a few things that will occur.

- On the first of every month your property manager will send you a rental statement. This usually coincides with rental income going into your bank account.
- At some date every month, interest will be charged by your bank. You might get a statement or might just view transactions online.
- Every three months you will pay water rates and council rates.
- Insurance is usually paid monthly or annually. Your broker will advise when your insurance needs to be updated.
- Your property manager will likely inspect your property twice a year and advise if any repairs are needed.
- Your tenant will probably be on a three-month, six-month, or twelve-month lease. The rent amount you charge should be reviewed every 12 months and, notwithstanding other factors, should increase by 5% per annum (in line with inflation), but the amount (more or less than this) is dictated by the market. You can look to increase the rent more by value-adding for the tenant (e.g. making cosmetic renovations, or adding a feature they would like) and negotiating for the rent to go higher.

Things to consider that you could use to leverage higher rent include: erecting a new shed, building a new carport, repainting, fitting a new kitchen, adding air-conditioning, replacing the carpet or allowing pets.

Renovation as a value-add strategy

If you are value-adding by renovating the property it is up to you whether this should be done before tenanting or later on. If you choose to value-add before you place your first tenant then it's worth getting your quotes during settlement or before exchange of contracts. This will certainly be the case if you know that renovating will allow a significantly higher rent and you are planning to buy and hold as a rental property. Have your team ready to renovate as soon as you settle on the property, with the goal to finish the renovation quickly, and get a tenant in and paying rent.

After the renovation is finished, if you determined that renovating will add capital value to the property, then you can look to refinance and pull out your cash to put into the next deal (provided the numbers support this). You may, however, need to wait three to six months for the bank to let you refinance.

The investor's role in property management

Your property manager will look after your property and tenant, so what does the investor need to do? There are a few tasks that can't be delegated.

- Receive your bills and pay them on time
- On a monthly basis, record your income and expenses into your accounting software or spreadsheet (see Chapter Sixteen) – or send this to your book-keeper
- Take phone calls from your property manager and make decisions on repairs, renovations, etc.
- Monitor your investment's profitability and cash flow and decide which investments to keep and which to sell (and what to buy next)
- Annually, submit a tax return (through your accountant).

The process, once you are used to it, is actually fairly straightforward. If you have successfully purchased and are now managing your first property, then consider buying another one!

What about selling?

Selling a property is something you will need to do to become a real property investor. People who buy and never sell are limited to what they can do.

We will cover profitable selling in the next book too!

CHAPTER NOTES AND ACTIONS

Before moving on to the conclusion, spend a few minutes writing down the things that resonated with you from this chapter.

What actions do you need to take, or what do you need to plan to do, to help you get to the next level in your investing?

Write down at least 5 things now.

1. _____
   _____
   _____

2. _____
   _____
   _____

3. _____
   _____
   _____

4. _____
   _____
   _____

5. _____
   _____
   _____

CONCLUSION

Congratulations on finishing this book. If, at the same time, you also managed to achieve the purchase of a property – especially if it was your first property – then congratulations again!

Only a small percentage of people ever become successful property investors with multiple properties and a sizeable portfolio. By getting to this stage you have made the first step in your journey as a property investor, well done.

Visit **www.achieveproperty.com/completed** and let us know what you have achieved.

We are very interested to hear what readers have done.

Next steps

The next step may be to move on to bigger and more creative deals, or multiple smaller ones. Bigger deals and creative deals have more complexity, but if you can handle a basic buy-reno-hold deal, then you can look at a more complicated renovation, or strata sub-division into the future.

Equally you can choose to buy smaller deals. There is merit in this strategy as well.

If you have followed the steps outlined here, hopefully you are in the position of being able to do a second or subsequent property deal in the near future.

Investors generally find that they can keep investing until they reach a ceiling where they have done as many deals as they can, and for some reason they hit a roadblock. This may be due to serviceability, available cash, limited time, or other reasons.

If this has happened to you, re-read Chapter Seventeen and consider working on your mindset, or re-read the specific chapter in this book that relates to the issue that is holding you back. There will be a way forward, you just need to figure out what it is for you, then take action!

My next book goes into more detail, following on with regard to how to build a multi-million-dollar property portfolio.

Bonus chapter

Just when you thought you had come to the end, I have decided to share with you a bonus chapter: "The Road Map to Grow Your Million-Dollar Portfolio".

This chapter is only available online – download it now from the homepage at **www.achieveproperty.com**.

I've been told it is the best chapter *not* in the book.

Enjoy this bonus chapter and good luck in your investing.

ANSWERS TO QUIZ QUESTIONS

Page 29
The amount of the first loan was 80% x $400,000 = $320,000
The amount of the second loan was 80% x $500,000 = $400,000
The equity released therefore was $400,000 – $320,000 = $80,000

Page 64
The initial interest cost (per annum) is $4,800
Maintenance cost (per annum) is $4,000
Rental income (per annum) is $10,000
Cash flow (per annum) is $1,200
With a possible rise in rates of 4% (conservatively high)
The new interest cost (per annum) is $8,000
The new maintenance cost (per annum) is $4,000
The new rental income (per annum) is $10,000
The new cash flow (per annum) is -$2,000

Page 91
Calculation: If a tenant pays $350 per week rent, and is 2.5 weeks in arrears, for a six-month period, what is the interest cost to the investor? (assume interest rate of 7%)?
Answer: $875 x 7% x 0.5 = $30.62

Page 109
(a) The price for buying the property $250,000
(b) Any purchase (closing) costs 5% = $12,500

(c) The costs of renovating the property 10% of purchase price =$25,000
(d) Any holding costs (for example the cost of the mortgage interest) 7% interest at an 80% LVR for 6 months = $7,000
(e) Agent commissions for sale (if you intend to sell) 4% of end-sale price = $12,800
Total cost = $307,300

DON'T FORGET THE BONUS TOOLS!

Before you leave us, a reminder to also download your **bonus property investing tools.** These three **exclusive** bonus downloads are guaranteed to help in your investing and are a thank you from us for reading our book.

Bonus 1   Twenty Rules for Successful Offers (valued at $79)

Bonus 2   Book-keeping Made Easy spreadsheet (valued at $39)

Bonus 3   Our Exclusive Offer Template (valued at $49)

To access these three great tools, use this link to register, **www.achieveproperty.com/bonus-registration**
and the password: **ToolsToUse.**

PLUS, remember you will find links to *all* the additional information outlined in this book, as well as a link to the tool download page, in one handy location at
www.achieveproperty.com/bonus-information.

(The link to download the bonus tools is at the bottom of this webpage.)

INDEX

accounting 149-150
adding value to property 100-101, 104-105, 186
affordability 77, 78
agents' commission 14
ANZ bank 39
applications for finance 44, 45
asset protection 140-141
average house prices 74-75

bank valuer 83
banks 39-40, 70, 102, 103
bonus chapter 190
bonus tools 193
book-keeping 150-152
book-keeping software 152-153
borrowing 39, 60, 141
budgeting 26
building inspections 14, 25, 127
buying property at the right price 116-117
buying your first investment property 169-187

capital expenses 155-156
capital gain 69, 101, 114
– realised 100
– unrealised 100
capital gains and losses 155
capital gains tax 30, 156-157
car loans 41
cash 45
cash flow 62-63, 89, 100, 101
cash rate 58-59, 60
Cashflow® 165
caveat emptor 124
closing costs 25
commercial finance 40, 43
Commonwealth Bank 39
companies 144
comparative sales prices 83
contracts for sale 128

conveyancing costs 13, 146
cost of buying versus renting 69
costs 25, 31, 110
Covey, R. Stephen 51
Covey's quadrant 51
credit cards 26, 27, 41
current market value 85

deals that don't stack up 44-45
debt 26, 41
de-cluttering 104, 106-107
decorating 106
delegating 54
deposits 25, 26, 31, 38, 70
depreciating allowances 110-111, 154
disadvantages of investing in property 11-14
discretionary trusts 141
due diligence 45, 124-130, 177

education 18, 160-162, 172
employment 43, 71
entry and exit costs 13-14
equity 28-29, 30, 45
exchanging contracts 179
expenses 26, 27

family trusts 141-142
filing 151-152
finance approval 44, 177-179
finance broker 39, 44
finding a good deal 173-175
first home owners grant 71, 72
first-time investors 124
fixed rates 62
focus 50-51
fractional reserve lending 102-103

general property investing education 162
global financial crisis (GFC) 11, 39, 62, 77

Index

government influences 70, 70-71
goods and services tax (GST) 72, 74-86

high rental yields 2, 18
high-cost assets 12-13
home-loan lenders 25
house price stability 77
house prices 67, 68, 69-70
housing bubble 77
housing markets 67
hurdles to property investing 21-24

illiquid assets 13
income 41
– from your property 42, 134-135
– increasing your 133-134
inflation 60
inspections 126-130
installment contracts 33, 34-35
insurance 91-92, 180
– building and contents 91-92
– premiums 14
interest rates 33, 42, 58-64, 70
– costs 100
– fluctuations 64
– historical range 61
– rises 62
interest-only loans 135-136
investment property – releasing equity in 30-31

joint venture partners 31-32, 134
"Journey's End" 6-7

Kiyosaki, Robert 165

land tax 157
landlord's insurance 91-92
landlording 89-97
landscaping 104, 105-106
learning strategies 163
lease options 33-34
legal fees 13, 25
legislation 34
lender's mortgage insurance (LMI) 28

lenders, types of 38-40
lending institution valuations 83
leverage 16-17, 70
liquidity 13
loan to value ratio (LVR) 27, 28, 43
loans – securing 40-42
local area inspections 127
long-term performance 17-18
low-market-value properties 119-120

maintenance and repairs 14
making an offer 119, 175-176
management costs 14-15
market crashes 17
market movements 78-79
market trends 76-78
median sale prices 74-75, 76, 78
mentoring 162-163
mindset 164
money partners 31, 32-33
mortgage brokers 39
mortgagee sales 121
my first property purchase 4-6

NAB 39
negative gearing 134
negotiating 85-86, 118, 175-176
no-money-down deals 33-35

operating expenses 155-156
oversupply 44
ownership in your own name 141

partnership agreement 32
partnerships 31-32, 46, 134, 142-143
passive income 21
PAYG tax 41
pest inspections 14, 25, 127
plumbing and electrical inspections 128-130
positive cash flow 2, 18
positive cash flow property 134, 135
positives of property investing 15-18
price 117, 118, 175-176
principal and interest loans 135-136

195

prioritising 52-55
private lending 32
procrastination 52-53
professional advice 157-158
profit 82
profit – calculating 108-109, 110
profitability 128
property courses 161
property growth reports 79
property investing simulation games 163
property investing technique education 162
property management 15-16, 90, 92-94, 95-96, 181, 183, 184, 186-187
property market 16-17
property professionals 171-172
property selection criteria 114-115, 171

quantity surveyors 110, 111

real estate agents 121
reason for investing 50
refinancing 101
regional Australia 18
renovating 104-105, 186
renovation costs 84
rent 15, 88
– paying on time 88-90
– arrears 89-91
rental yield 69, 83
repayments 60
– ability to service 41
Reserve Bank of Australia (RBA) 58, 59, 60
residential finance 43
residential property 16, 27
risk 43-44
risk tolerance 63-64

saving 26
scalability 17
search engines 121-122
second mortgage 46
secure asset 16

self managed super funds (SMSFs) 72, 144-145
self-employed 41
sellers 82, 118, 119
selling a property 30, 120, 187
seminars 165
serviceability 41, 133
– calculators 42
– ceiling 42
settlement 181-182, 183-184
Seven Habits of Highly Effective People, The 51
share trading 17
shares 12, 13
software 79, 85, 121-122, 152
solicitors 146, 182
sourcing finance 69
stamp duty 13, 25
standard variable rates 58, 59, 60, 61
structuring 139-147, 157
subdivision 104, 107-108
supply and demand 60, 68-69, 71, 77
supply of money 72

tax 140, 142, 146, 153-154
television 53-54
tenants 15, 30, 88
– incentives 95
– managing 94-95
time management 51-52
time partner 31
time to invest 49-55

undersupply of property 16, 18
US housing market 68

valuations 82, 84
valuation software 85, 173
value 82, 110, 172-173
vendor finance 34, 46

water rates 14, 15
websites 120
Westpac 39

Printed by Libri Plureos GmbH in Hamburg, Germany